A to Zany
Community Activities

A to Zany Community Activities for Students of English

Lynn Stafford-Yilmaz

Ann Arbor

THE UNIVERSITY OF MICHIGAN PRESS

Copyright © by the University of Michigan 1998
ISBN 0-472-08501-8
Library of Congress Catalog Card No. 97-80102
Published in the United States of America by
The University of Michigan Press
Manufactured in the United States of America

2001   2000   1999   1998   4   3   2   1

This book is dedicated to my students and teachers, who have shown me both the world and my own backyard.

Acknowledgments

I would like to thank my colleagues and students, who have given me nonstop energy, fresh ideas, and steady enthusiasm during the development of this text. In particular, this book has grown from the experiences of international students of the Saitama YMCA and from input of immigrant and refugee students at Bellevue Community College in Washington State.

Also at the Bellevue Community College, Garnet Templin-Imel modeled tenacity together with an indispensable sense of humor throughout the writing phase. My husband, Mustafa Yilmaz, served as a frontline sounding board on the practicality and interest of each activity in this book to nonnatives of the United States. At the American Cultural Exchange in Seattle, Ede Courtenay and Betsy Hudson deserve a cheerful thanks for their constant, friendly interest in the creation of *A to Zany Community Activities for Students of English*. As well, fellow instructors of the American Cultural Exchange, Eve L. Connell at the Monterey Institute of International Studies, and Kelly Sippell at the University of Michigan Press gave me the initial thumbs-up that jump-started this project.

Even more fundamentally, my thanks go to my parents, Donna and Shannon Stafford. As well, the Monterey Institute of International Studies, and the many fine instructors there, have given me the confidence to apply what research is teaching us in bold and energizing ways.

Outside of the ESL community, this book received tremendous benefit from a team of highly skilled, flexible, and astute photographers: Jan Bogle, Joe Budne, Cynthia Canning, Davis Freeman, Craig Huber, Larry Kezner, Mary Levin, Officer Tami McClincy, Sean G. Scholey, Corky Trewin, and Robert West put together their cameras and their creativity in a fine complement of artwork that should really be in a book of its own. Also, thanks to David Johnson for his assistance and support in locating photographers.

Among our models, thanks go to Maria Aguilar, Marsha Butler, Denise Crawford, Michael K. Duncan, Colin Glidden, Dorothy C. Hansen, Hercules, Bryce Kipp, La Cocina del Puerco, Officer Gary Lindell, Officer Greg Neubert, Ashley Scholey, the Seattle Seahawks, Angela Smith, Ann Stafford, Paul Trebach, and Andy Weinstein.

A Note to Users of This Book

A to Zany Community Activities presents students with twenty-six community-based activities using the English alphabet as a framework. These activities have been designed for low-intermediate to advanced ESL students. The purpose of these activities is to draw learners out of the classroom and into the local area where they can interact purposefully with one of the best classrooms—the community.

Text Organization

Each community assignment begins with a short activity designed to stimulate discussion, to activate background knowledge, and to prepare students for the activity itself.

Most activities have been designed to last about two hours. This includes student research into transportation, hours of operation, and other logistical details. Activities make excellent homework assignments for learners in any setting, and they can be used to enhance all English programs. While many of the activities can be done in pairs or small groups, others are just as effective when done individually.

Each community activity is followed by discussion and information synthesis. This takes about thirty minutes of class time.

For learners who are interested, several optional follow-up activities are proposed in each chapter. Learners may work on these individually or in pairs. These optional activities require varying amounts of time. Most are done outside of class, but some include in-class demonstrations or work. Many of the optional activities have the potential to be stand-alone activities, according to learners' individual interests and pursuits.

This book is designed to serve as both a standard workbook and as a scrapbook. As a workbook, each activity in *A to Zany* is followed by a short glossary with new vocabulary that is relevant to the theme of the activity. Glossed vocabulary words are in bold type in the text. All activities also include space for students to write their answers and assignments.

Additionally, *A to Zany* is a scrapbook for learners. As a keepsake, it holds brochures, ticket stubs, photographs, and other mementos of U.S. culture that students can look back on when (and if) they return to their own countries. It is anticipated that learners will save this book as a diary of their language progress and cultural growth.

Audience

With its emphasis on learner independence, communicative interaction, and comparative reflection, *A to Zany* is particularly useful for young adults and adult learners of English. *A to Zany* incorporates a balance of class work, group activities, pair work, and individual tasks, addressing various different learning styles and benefiting from the merits of all possible class groupings.

Independent learners of English in the United States will also find *A to Zany* an ideal tool for stimulating language interaction. The language and cultural opportunities in this book are rich and varied, and they do not require a formal classroom setting for successful and rewarding use.

Text Length

A to Zany can be used in a language course of virtually any length. It is not anticipated that any one user will complete the entire book. For a variety of reasons, some activities will be more appropriate than will others for any given group of learners. For example, some communities will have better access to some of the destinations in this book. Also, each student population will have its own level of interest in the different activities. In addition, time, transportation, and even weather, may determine which activities you choose.

For these reasons, this book intentionally contains more than any one learner is expected to do. As a suggested guideline, you might think of doing one activity per week. In a ten-week class, then, you would complete ten units in the book. The completion of nine to twenty activities is considered successful utilization of this workbook.

Also, it is not necessary that learners complete every step in every activity of this book. One of the exceptional features of *A to Zany* is that it can be easily adapted to meet learners' specific needs and interests.

Skills

• • • • •

The primary skills that are practiced in this book are speaking, listening, observing, analyzing, comparing, and critical thinking; the secondary skills are reading, writing, and researching. Based in many of the philosophies of content-based language teaching, *A to Zany*'s content area is that of culture. This book is not a grammar book, although it can be used to enhance a grammar text or grammar-based syllabus. (See the table "Integrating *A to Zany* into the Grammar-Based or Functional Syllabus" on page xiv.)

In addition to the opportunities for language, culture, and general educational development, *A to Zany* also encourages learners' active observation of, and participation in, U.S. culture. This firsthand participation in everyday society both broadens and deepens users' cross-cultural experience in the United States. These activities are specifically designed to empower learners within their communities—one of the key goals of the book.

In more ways than one, *A to Zany* falls outside standard categories of ESL texts. *A to Zany* focuses on the learner in his or her community—and on the intense, evolving relationship between the two—as the center of the cross-cultural and language learning experience. Given this position of the learner, it is natural that the classroom, the teacher, and the text itself take on quite different roles than they have held in the traditional ESL classroom.

Given this approach, users of this book are encouraged to take as much responsibility as they can for each activity. Checking hours of operation, figuring out bus schedules, finding information in the phone book, setting dates, and managing logistics are as much a part of the language learning process as the activities themselves. As much as possible, these tasks should be performed by students themselves.

To the Teacher

• • • • • • • • • • • • • • • •

It is not necessary, or even desirable, to start with the first chapter or to work in order. It is recommended that you and your students choose to do the activities that interest you the most. If you are using this text as a supplement, the tables on pages xiv–xv will serve as good guides for what chapters are most complementary to your syllabus.

When using *A to Zany,* the teacher's primary role is to help steer students in their planning and research. Where planning is necessary, it is almost always the learners' responsibility and should be considered a central part of the learning process.

As a teacher, however, you should be aware of a few special considerations when using this book. First and foremost consider *safety*. You should use your own discretion and encourage students to use theirs in doing the activities in this book. (Also, see the disclaimer, page xiii.)

Second, be aware that some activities in *A to Zany* assume a certain degree of boldness on the learner's part. For example, in the D activity, learners are asked to make a conversational observation to a dog owner about his or her dog, such as, "Your dog is cute." Students should not be forced into uncomfortable communicative situations. If a student does not want to do a specific activity, or take a specific step in one of the activities, this is perfectly acceptable. In such cases, however, the learner should be encouraged to propose an alternative.

Last, it is noteworthy that some activities require money for things such as transportation and entrance fees. The estimated cost of each activity is marked in the Prep & Preview section of each activity.

Author's Wish

I have compiled various personal and professional experiences in creating a tool that will bring hours of meaningful communication into our classrooms and into learners' lives. I hope that you will enjoy these activities as much as my learners and I have. Every time we use one of these activities, we learn something new about the book itself. You, as users of this book, may also see ways that *A to Zany* can be improved. On such occasions, it would be my pleasure to receive your input. After all, teachers and learners are the best critics around. You can reach me, via the publisher, at:

> Lynn Stafford-Yilmaz
> c/o The University of Michigan Press
> 839 Greene Street
> P.O. Box 1104
> Ann Arbor, Michigan 48106-1104

Disclaimer

This book is designed to structure communicative activities for ESL students in their community and with native speakers of English. Students and teachers should use their own discretion in working on these activities. Given possible safety concerns, and given the newness of many ESL students to the United States, students should be instructed in basic safety awareness in the United States before using this book. Activity P, which includes a police presentation in the ESL classroom, may be a good starting point for such safety instruction.

It is suggested that teachers review each chapter before assigning it. The teacher may use his/her knowledge of the area to gauge the safety and usefulness of each activity. In addition, when assigning activities from this book, teachers should consider making such assignments optional. Students should understand that it is their complete option to abandon any activity if they feel unsafe, unsure, or uncomfortable in any way.

It may also be advisable for students to work in pairs, especially if students are younger. This book is not recommended for use by children.

The purpose of this workbook is to structure language learning opportunities for ESL students in the community and/or with the public. The author and the University of Michigan Press shall have neither the liability nor responsibility to any person or entity with respect to any loss or damage caused, or alleged to be caused, directly or indirectly, by the activities suggested in this book. If you do not wish to be bound by the above, you may return this book to the publisher within 60 days of purchase, in new condition, for a full refund.

TABLE 1.   Integrating *A to Zany* into the Grammar-Based or Functional Syllabus

You are studying . . .	especially good activities are . . .
Comparatives	A = art, B = ball games, D = dogs, E = edible, F = Fahrenheit, G = garage sales, J = jobs, O = older adults, Q = quick stuff, R = restaurants, T = television
Conditionals	E = edible, G = garage sales, K = kissing, W = wheelchairs
Employment	J = jobs, P = police, U = universities, V = volunteers
Entertainment	A = art, B = ball games, H = holidays, L = local, M = movies, N = newspapers, R = restaurants, T = television, Z = zoo
Expressing agreement and disagreement	B = ball games, E = edible, J = jobs, K = kissing, L = local, N = newspapers, R = restaurants, Y = your activity
Expressing likes and dislikes	A = art, E = edible, H = holidays, K = kissing, L = local, O = older adults, M = movies, N = newspapers
Family life	D = dogs, G = garage sales, H = holidays, K = kissing, O = older adults, S = supermarkets, T = television
Food	E = edible, R = restaurants, S = supermarkets
Future Time	O = older adults
Government	H = holidays, I = indigenous people, J = jobs, N = newspapers, P = police, U = universities, W = wheelchairs, X = xenophilia
Modal Auxiliaries	J = jobs, F = Fahrenheit, K = kissing, P = police, X = xenophilia, Y = your activity
Past Time	C = churches, I = indigenous people, G = garage sales, J = jobs, K = kissing, L = local, N = newspapers, O = older adults, R = restaurants, T = television
Present Perfect	D = dogs, H = holidays, M = movies, O = older adults, P = police, V = volunteers
Present Time	A = art, B = ball games, C = churches, D = dogs, F = Fahrenheit, H = holidays, J = jobs, K = kissing, L = local, M = movies, N = newspapers, P = police, Q = quick stuff, R = restaurants, U = universities, V = volunteers, W = wheelchairs, Y = your activity, Z = zoo
Sports	B = ball games, H = holidays, J = jobs, L = local, N = newspapers, U = universities, V = volunteers
Wh-questions	A = art, B = ball games, C = churches, D = dogs, E = edible, F = Fahrenheit, G = garage sales, H = holidays, I = indigenous people, J = jobs, K = kissing, L = local, P = police, R = restaurants, T = television, U = universities, V = volunteers, X = xenophilia, Y = your activity, Z = zoo

TABLE 2. Integrating *A to Zany* into a Skill-Based Curriculum

You want practice with . . .	especially good activities are . . .
Listening and observing	A = art, B = ball games, C = churches, D = dogs, E = edible, F = Fahrenheit, G = garage sales, H = holidays, J = jobs, K = kissing, L = local, M = movies, O = older adults, P = police, Q = quick stuff, S = supermarkets, T = television, U = universities, V = volunteers, W = wheelchairs, X = xenophilia, Z = zoo
Speaking	A = art, B = ball games, C = churches, D = dogs, F = Fahrenheit, G = garage sales, H = holidays, J = jobs, L = local, P = police, Q = quick stuff, R = restaurants, U = universities, V = volunteers, X = xenophilia, Y = your activity, Z = zoo
Reading	A = art, H = holidays, I = indigenous people, L = local, M = movies, N = newspapers, R = restaurants, S = supermarkets, T = television
Writing	A = art, B = ball games, C = churches, H = holidays, I = indigenous people, J = jobs, K = kissing, L = local, M = movies, P = police, X = xenophilia, Y = your activity

TABLE 3. Adapting *A to Zany* to Your Learners' Needs

You or your class are . . .	especially good activities are . . .
Advanced beginners to early intermediate	A = art, D = dogs, E = edible, F = Fahrenheit, G = garage sales, H = holidays, K = kissing, L = local, N = newspapers, O = older adults, P = police, Q = quick stuff, R = restaurants, S = supermarkets, U = universities, W = wheelchairs, Y = your activity, Z = zoo
Intermediate to advanced	All activities
Brand new to the United States or to the area	L = local, P = police, R = restaurants, S = supermarkets
Mostly monocultural	D = dogs, F = Fahrenheit, G = garage sales, H = holidays, I = indigenous people, J = jobs, L = local, M = movies, N = newspapers, O = older adults, P = police, R = restaurants, S = supermarkets, T = television, U = universities, V = volunteers, W = wheelchairs, X = xenophilia, Y = your activity, Z = zoo
Multicultural	All activities

Contents

Activity

A   Art   1

B   Ball Games   8

C   Churches, Mosques,

Synagogues, and Temples   16

D   Dogs   25

E   Edible Things   33

F   Fahrenheit   41

G   Garage Sales   48

H   Holidays   55

I   Indigenous People   63

J   Jobs   71

K   Kissing   80

L   The Local Connection   87

M   Movies   93

Activity

N   Newspapers   98

O   Older Adults   104

P   Police   109

Q   Quick Stuff   116

R   Restaurants   123

S   Supermarkets   130

T   Television   137

U   Universities   144

V   Volunteers   151

W   Wheelchairs   159

X   Xenophilia   165

Y   Your Activity   174

Z   Zoo   180

Art

At the Metropolitan Museum of Art in New York City, viewers look at a sculpture.

Prep & Preview
· · · · · · · · · · · · · · ·

You will need the arts or entertainment section from a local newspaper. In class, you will need a standard, English-language dictionary. You will attend one art show.
Cost: Free to $3.00.

Before the Activity
· ·

1. Think about art. What do you think art is? Write your own definition of this word.

    _____

    _____

2. Look up the word *art* in an English dictionary. Write the definition here. (You do not need to copy every word.)

    _____

    _____

3. When you think of art, what do you think of? (Try to think "in English" when you think of the English word *art*.) _____

    _____

4. What is the word for *art* in your language? _____

5. When you think of *art* in your language, what do you think of?

    _____

    _____

6. Have you bought art in America? If so, what did you buy? _____

    _____

7. What's the difference between a **gallery** and a **museum?** _____

    _____

8. Have you ever been to an art show in your country? If so, write about it.

    _____

    _____

9. There are two broad types of art: performing arts and visual arts. Write down two more examples of each:

   Performing arts: _ballet_ _____

   Visual arts: _sculpture_ _____

10. What is your favorite type of art, and why?

    _____

    _____

    _____

11. Read through the activity that follows. Make sure that you understand it. You may work with a classmate or ask your teacher if you have questions.

Everyone enjoys art in a different way.

Photo by Joe Budne

The Activity
. . . .

1. From the newspaper, choose an art show (visual art) that you would like to attend. Paste the newspaper notice here or copy its information. (Include the name and date of the newspaper.)

2. Call the art gallery or museum you will go to. Find out the hours the gallery or museum is open. Ask if there are tours or if there is a **docent** who can show you around. Ask for the times of tours.

    Hours _____

    Tour times _____

3. Go to the art show.

4. Date you attended _____

5. Name of current show(s) _____

6. Media or **medium** (for example, watercolors, oils, or wood) _____

7. Name your favorite piece of art and artist _____

    _____

8. Describe the piece of art that you liked _____

    _____

    _____

9. Why did you like it the most? _____

    _____

CULTURE NUGGET

In 1863, Napoléon III ordered a special display of pictures that had previously been rejected by a popular **exhibition.** Among the artists were Manet, Pissarro, Whistler, and Cézanne. The special display was called the Salon des Refuses. (Reginald G. Haggar, *A Dictionary of Art Terms* [New York: Hawthorn Books, 1962], 168.)

10. Name your least favorite piece of art and the artist _____

_____

11. Why was it your least favorite? _____

_____

12. Describe it. _____

_____

13. Ask the receptionist if biographical information about the artists is available, and if there is a free brochure on the museum/gallery. Staple the information to this page.

14. Did you take a guided tour? If so, write down some of your thoughts about the tour. _____

_____

_____

_____

15. If there is a gift shop, take some time to go inside and look around. If there is a postcard that would remind you of your day in this art museum or gallery, buy it. Staple it to this page.

After the Activity

1. Look at *your* definition of art in the first activity. Using your definition, was the show that you saw art? Why or why not?

_____

2.   Using the definition in the English dictionary, was it art? Why or why not?

_____

_____

_____

3.   Read one of the artist's biographies that you got at the museum. Think about the artist's background. Think about the art that you saw. Could you see the artist's background reflected in his/her art? If so, how? (For example, an artist who has lived through a war may create art that reflects his or her wartime experiences.)

_____

_____

_____

4.   Do art museums in your country have docents? _____

5.   If you have been to an art show in your country, what was similar and what was different between that art show and this art show? (If you have never been to an art show in your country, you should skip this question.)

_____

_____

_____

6.   In groups of three or four, tell your classmates about the art show you attended. Tell them what you liked and did not like, and tell them any interesting observations you made.

7.   Show your classmates your postcard or museum information.

Optional Activities
. . . .

•   Read a review in a newspaper or local magazine of the show you saw.

•   Write your own review of the show. Give it to your teacher to look at. Then, staple it on the back of this page.

- Read about some other artists who were featured in the show. After reading about them, do you understand their art better?

- If you have art skills that you would like to show, teach, or perform in your class, especially of arts from your native country, talk to your teacher. Choose a class time when you can share your skill. (Ask a classmate to take your picture in action. Paste that picture in this book.)

- Go to another art show. Compare the two shows. Tell your classmates about your experience.

- Go to a show of the performing arts. (You may find inexpensive shows at a local university or performing arts school.) Write about the differences and similarities that you observed in these art forms.

- Choose five to ten words from this chapter that are new for you. Write the words and write your own sentences using these words.

GLOSSARY

docent, noun	A tour guide and lecturer, as at a museum.
exhibition, noun	A public show.
gallery, noun	A place for showing and selling artworks.
medium, noun	Any material used in art.
museum, noun	A place for preserving and showing artistic, historical, or scientific objects.

B

Ball Games

Photo courtesy of Corky Trewin/Seattle Seahawks

In America, football is different from soccer. The Seattle Seahawks, a
football team in the National Football League (NFL), look tough.

Prep & Preview

· · · · · · · · · · · · · · · ·

Using local newspapers or community mailings, find lists of local ball games—football, baseball, or basketball, for example. High school, community college, little **league,** or **youth** club games are often free. You will go to a game. Bring several sports sections of a few newspapers to class.

Cost: Price of a newspaper to price of game.

Before the Activity

· · · · · · · · · · · · · · · · · · ·

1. List the four most popular types of ball games in your country (if you're not sure, just guess).

    _____

2. Can you think of any ball games that are popular in your country, but not in many other countries? If so, write down the name of one game and its description.

    _____

    _____

    _____

    _____

3. Talk to two classmates. Ask if they have heard about the game you described in question 2. Tell them about the game.

4. Listen to information about their games. Write the name of the games and a short description.

    _____

    _____

    _____

5. In American English, "football" refers to the game with an oval-shaped brown ball and many large men wearing **helmets.** America is one of the few countries where football is played. Football is played in Canada, but the **rules** are slightly different. Have you ever seen a football game? In groups of

three or four students, try to write down as many things as you know about American or Canadian football. For example, how many players are there on a team? How does a team win points? Have you seen women playing football?

_____

_____

_____

_____

6. As a class, share your information on football. Put all of your information on the chalkboard. Your teacher may be able to add information.

CULTURE NUGGET American football actually started in the mid-1800s and evolved from rugby. In its early years, football was so dangerous that many colleges did not allow students to play, including Harvard University. In 1905, for example, 18 college and high school football players were killed playing the sport. This led President Theodore Roosevelt to suggest the start of a **regulatory** commission for college football. Today, this commission is called the National Collegiate Athletic Association (NCAA). Now there is a commission for professional football, too: the National Football League (NFL). (Ralph Hickok, _Encyclopedia of North American Sports History_ [New York: Facts on File, 1992].)

7. In the United States, each team sport has a season. For example, football is a fall sport. Look at the sports section of your newspaper. Can you guess what sport season it is now?

8. Read one article in the newspaper about a ball game that interests you. Circle three or four new words in the article. Guess what they mean, and then look them up in a dictionary. Staple the article here.

9. As a class, put together your information about upcoming ball games in your area. You may use newspapers, mailings, or personal information. Write the games, times, and locations on the chalkboard.

10. Choose a game that you would like to attend. A high school or college game might be fun. Try to think of an American you know who might be interested in going to the game; maybe he or she will go with you.

11. Read through the activity that follows. Make sure you understand it. You may work with a classmate, or ask your teacher if you have questions.

The Activity
. . . .

1. Make your plans to go to the ball game. If you know an American who's interested in going to the game, invite that person. Find out if you need tickets for the game. If so, get tickets. You should be able to buy tickets for high school games at the event, but you may need to purchase tickets for college games in advance.

2. Game location and date _____

3. Team names _____

4. Name of sport _____

5. Before the game starts, talk to an American about the game. Ask him or her a few questions about the sport. If it is a sport you don't know much about, ask an American about the rules. If you know the sport, ask him or her about American customs that go with the sport. (For example, ask them about "tailgate parties" or "the wave," which are usually associated with American football. Or, ask about special vocabulary that goes with the sport.)

6. Write down at least four things, or words, that you learned about the sport.

_____

_____

_____

_____

7. Go to the game. Listen for new sports words. They might be words that you circled in the newspaper article or that an American told you about. If you hear the word, write it down. (If you don't hear those words, write down other new words that you hear at the game.)

    _____

    _____

    _____

8. Describe the game. Could you follow the rules? Could you understand the **announcer**s? Was the game indoors or outdoors? How many fans were there? Was it like a ball game in your own country? Who won the game, and what was the final score?

    _____

    _____

    _____

    _____

    Who won _____

    The score (put the winning score first) _____

9. If you got a ticket or a program, paste it here.

Basketball is a popular winter sport in the United States. This is a high school game.

After the Activity

1. In a large group, tell your classmates about the game that you attended. Compare your observations.

2. In your group, talk about **spectator** sports in your own country. Have you ever gone to a **competitive** ball game in your country? If so, talk about it.

3. How are spectator sports different in your country from sports in the United States? Write down your impressions.

   _____

   _____

   _____

   _____

4. Again, read the article on a ball game that you stapled in this book.

5. Write your own article or story about the game you saw.

6. Give your article or story to another student to read. Read that student's article.

7. Staple your article or story into this book.

Optional Activities
. . . .

•   Form a group of students who want to play football. Find a football player, or somebody who knows the sport well, who can help you or teach you how to play. (Many American students at many levels of school—grade school, high school, college—play football. They may be willing to help you.) Borrow a football from the school sports center or from your teacher. Play the game.

•   Watch a ball game on TV. Listen for your new sports vocabulary. As you watch, try to learn two new rules in the game.

•   Go to the library. Read about the history of one sport. Write a short report. Share it with your class.

•   Teach your class how to play a ball game from your country. Play it.

•   As a class, invent a ball game. Make teams. Make rules. Choose a ball. Play it.

- Attend a game of a different sport. Compare your experiences.

- Go to a professional ball game, a women's ball game, or some other sporting event that you have not attended before.

- Choose five to ten words from this chapter that are new for you. Write the words and write your own sentences using these words.

GLOSSARY

announcer, noun	A person who says something publicly.
competitive, adj.	Relating to a contest between two or more people.
helmet, noun	A hard hat that protects your head.
league, noun	A group of people with a specific interest.
regulate, verb	To manage or control.
rule, verb	An official instruction about what you can or cannot do.
spectator, noun	Someone who watches an event but does not participate in it.
youth, adj., noun	A time in life between 13 and 18 years of age; a person of that age.

C

Churches, Mosques, Synagogues, and Temples

Photo by Joe Budne

Have you ever been inside a church? a synagogue? a temple? a mosque?

16

Prep & Preview
· · · · · · · · · · · · · · · ·

Get the names and addresses of a few churches, mosques, or other religious centers near your school. You will attend a **service.** Note: Your teacher can help you choose established, respected, **mainstream institution**s. Some organizations, known as **cult**s, are not safe to visit, even once. Cost: Free to optional donation.

Before the Activity
· · · · · · · · · · · · · · · · · · · ·

1. Write down the name of every religion that you know of. (If you don't know the English word, you can write it in your language.)

    _____

    _____

    _____

2. Most world religions have a place for **worship,** such as a church, mosque, synagogue, or temple. Have you ever been in one of these buildings? If so, which one(s)?

    _____

    _____

3. Think of the religious centers you have visited. Or, think of centers for worship that you have seen on television or in movies. What are some of the common features of these buildings? For example, most religious centers have a large area for sitting or **kneel**ing. Many have candles or **incense.** Many have art. Make a list of other common features. (You may use words from your native language.)

    _____

    _____

    _____

    _____

CULTURE NUGGET Fire is commonly used in religions. Fire has the power both to aid and to destroy. People are fascinated by fire's flame. From the holy writing of Brahmanic Hinduism dating to the first millenium B.C., to the Aztec and Incas, through modern Christianity, fire has been used as a religious symbol. Throughout history, many places of worship have used lamps and candles. If you worship somewhere, are candles used? (*The Encyclopedic Dictionary of Religion,* Eds., Meagher, Paul K., Thomas O'Brien, and Sister Consuelo Aherne. Washington D.C.: Corpus Publications, 1979.)

4. Talk to a classmate and compare your lists in question 3. Then you can make a list together.

5. As a class, share your lists from question 3. Make complete lists on the chalkboard.

6. Even though there are many different religions, there are similarities among many of them. One similarity may be the features in the center for worship. Why do you think that the buildings for so many different religions have such similar features? Choose three specific items that are similar from your class list (question 5). Write down why you think each is a common feature in religious buildings.

    _____

    _____

    _____

CULTURE NUGGET There are many different Christian churches. For example, Episcopalian, Methodist, Presbyterian, and Baptist churches are all Christian. They are Christian because they all believe that Jesus Christ is God. Even though they are all Christian, some of their beliefs and practices vary. (*The Encyclopedic Dictionary of Religion,* Eds., Meagher, Paul K., Thomas O'Brien, and Sister Consuelo Aherne. Washington D.C.: Corpus Publications, 1979.)

7. Read through the activity that follows. Make sure you understand it. You may work with a classmate or ask your teacher if you have questions.

The Activity

· · · · · · · · · · · · · ·

1. Find a religious worship center that you can visit. You might talk to a friend, or look in the yellow pages in the phone book under "church," "mosque," "synagogue," or "temple." You may want to do this activity with another classmate or with a friend. (Try to find a center whose religion is not common in your own country.) Find out the hours of the center's service. Find out if nonmembers of the religious group can visit.

2. Name of center and address _____

3. Hours/days of services _____

4. Religion _____

5. Go to a religious service at the center.

6. Date of your visit _____

7. Describe the building, both inside and outside. _____

    _____

    _____

    _____

8. List the physical features that you see in this religious building and that you had also written down in preactivity question 3.

    _____

    _____

9. Describe the service. Was there a main speaker? If so, was it a man or a woman? What was the topic of the speaker's speech?

    _____

    _____

    _____

10. How many people attended the service (guess)? Was there music? If so, describe it.

_____

_____

_____

_____

11. What was the general mood of the service? For example, was it cheerful? Serious? Thoughtful?

_____

_____

_____

12. Was a book read during the service? If so, do you know the name of the book?

_____

13. What language(s) was/were used in the service? _____

14. Did people move their hands, heads, eyes, or bodies in patterns that you haven't seen before? If so, what did they do? Can you guess why they did it?

_____

_____

_____

15.   After the service, walk through the room where the service was held. Try to find something that you have never seen before or that you don't understand. Draw a picture of it here.

16.   Many religious centers have inexpensive religious items for sale, such as bookmarks, plastic beads, or **prayer**s. Many have free brochures or small prayer sheets. Find something that you like, and staple it here.

17.   Go to the next section and do tasks 1 and 2 before your next class.

After the Activity

1.   Talk to an American, or to one of your classmates, who knows about the religion of the service you attended. You could even talk to somebody at the service. Ask him or her a couple of questions. For example, if there was a book used during the service, find out who wrote it or its origin. Ask about the hand or body movements that the service members used. Ask about the fundamental beliefs of members of that religion. Ask about the item that you drew in task 15 in the previous section. Write the questions you asked and the answers you received.

_____

_____

_____

_____

_____

_____

2.   Ask an American person to name every religion that he or she knows of. Write them down. How many are there? Compare the answers to yours in task 1 in the beginning of this chapter.

_____

_____

_____

3.   In small groups with your classmates, talk about the services you attended.

4.   Listen to your classmates' experiences. Write down the religion of the centers they visited. Write down two new things you learned about each religion.

Religion _____

_____

_____

_____

Religion _____

_____

_____

_____

Religion _____

_____

_____

_____

5. Based on what you have learned, can you tell which religious group gathers in which building? Try to match them.

Jews	Mosque
Moslems	Temple
Buddhists	Church
Christians	Synagogue

Optional Activities

. . . .

*   Read in an encyclopedia about a religion that isn't common in your own country. Write a short report about it. Staple it in this book.

*   Attend another service at the same religious center. See if you notice different things. Compare the services.

*   Attend a service at a center that one of your classmates attended.

*   Read the headline of every article in the newspaper for one day. How many articles are related to religion?

*   If you practice a religion yourself, think about this: If a foreigner came to your country and visited a service of your religion, what things might confuse or surprise the foreigner? Make a list.

*   If you practice a religion that has an upcoming holiday, make a presentation about that holiday to your class. If there are special foods, music, dancing, or customs connected to the religious day or days, tell your classmates about it or perform the customs.

*   Choose five to ten words from this chapter that are new for you. Write the words and write your own sentences using these words.

GLOSSARY

cult, noun	A strong devotion, which seems religious, to a person, thing or idea.
incense, noun	A substance that gives a pleasant odor when burned.
institution, noun	An organization where people work together.
kneel, verb	To bend one's legs with the knees to the ground.
mainstream, adj.	Something that is common or regular.
prayer, noun	An expression to God.
service, noun	A religious meeting.
worship, verb	To express devotion.

D

Dogs

True love between a man and his dog.

Prep & Preview   You will spend time in public, observing dogs and
. . . .   talking to dog owners.
Cost: Free!

Before the Activity
. . . .

1. Do you have a dog? If so, describe him or her.

_____

_____

2. Think about dogs in your country. What is your image of dogs in your
    country? Are they cute, cuddly house pets? Or are they hungry street
    wanderers?

_____

_____

_____

3. In many countries, certain animals are highly respected and some are even
    revered. Other animals are considered low or dirty. What animals are "high"
    in your country? Which are "low"? Make a list. Where are dogs on your list?
    Why do you think these animals ended up with these positions?

_____

_____

_____

4. In English, we have many idioms and expressions that refer to dogs. For
    example, somebody might say to a friend of theirs, "You old dog." A very
    tired person might say, "I'm dog tired." We also say, "Dog is man's best
    friend." There are the direct comments, "You have dog breath" and "You
    can't teach an old dog a new trick." A popular phrase about competitiveness
    is "It's a dog-eat-dog world." Regarding the weather, you might hear "It's
    raining cats and dogs." What do these expressions tell you about the
    American view of dogs, and why?

_____

_____

_____

5. Do you have any expressions referring to dogs in your language? What are they?

_____

_____

_____

6. In the Middle East, if you want to insult somebody, you can say to them, "You're a dog, and you're the son of a dog, too." What does this expression tell you about the way dogs are viewed in the Middle East?

_____

_____

_____

7. In America, many dogs are considered to be members of the family. Many dogs live in a family home. Some have their own bed. They go on diets if they get too fat. They wear hand-knit sweaters. They stay in special hotels for dogs. Some dogs have surgery that may be as expensive or more expensive than surgery for humans. In some cities, dogs may ride on public transportation, but they must pay the bus fare, too! In small groups, discuss these points.

8. Read through the activity that follows. Make sure that you understand it. You may work with a classmate, or ask your teacher if you have questions.

Photo by Larry Kezner

Not all dogs get a place at the table!

The Activity
. . . .

1. Go out in public in one afternoon and watch dog owners.

2. Write about three dogs that you see, and write about their owners. Do you notice anything interesting that you would probably not see in your own country?

   _____

   _____

   _____

   _____

   _____

   _____

3. Some people think that pets and owners often look like each other. Did you

   notice this? _____

_____

_____

4. Americans seem to like to talk about their dogs. In fact, total strangers on the street may start chatting about a dog.

5. Start a conversation with one of the dog owners you see. Start with, "Your dog is very _____ (big, cute, well **behave**d)." Try to talk with the owner about the dog for at least a minute. Be ready with a follow-up question. For example: "Do you take your dog to **obedience** school?" "Is your dog a he or a she?" "How long have you had him or her?"

6. Take a few simple notes about the conversation. Be prepared to tell your classmates about it.

_____

_____

_____

_____

7. Interview an American dog owner whom you know. Ask these questions. Write two more questions of your own, and ask them too.

Dog's name _____

Owner's name _____

How long have you had your dog? _____

What's your dog's last name? _____

Does your dog have his own house? _____

Does your dog take vitamins? _____

Who exercises more, you or your dog? _____

If you had another life, would you want to be your dog? Why or why

not? _____

_____

_____

Write two of your own questions below.

_____

_____

_____

_____

After the Activity
· · · · · · · · · · · · · · · · · ·

1.   In small groups, tell your classmates about your observations of dogs and their owners.

2.   Tell your group about your talk with a dog-owner, from task 5.

3.   Tell your group about your interview with the American dog-owner, from task 7.

4.   Compare your answers.

CULTURE Sales of dog products in the United States totaled $668 million dollars in 1994. Of this, over 90 million went to dog snacks. ("From Jeweled Collars to Snow Shoes, Dog Products Mean Business," **NUGGET** _Detroit Free Press,_ 22 January 1996, F6.)

5.   What are some of the more popular pets in your country? _____

_____

6.   In Japan, some people keep **beetle**s as pets. What are some pets unique to

your country? _____

7.   In your group, tell your classmates about pets in your country.

8. In general, what do you think are some of the difficulties in having a pet? Talk about it in small groups.

9. In general, what do you think are some of the joys of having a pet? Talk about it in your group.

Optional Activities

· · · · · · · · · · · · · · · · · · · ·

•   Visit an animal **shelter.** (This may be an emotionally difficult task.)

•   Call an animal hotel in your town. Check the rates for a medium-sized dog or for a cat for one night. Report your findings to your classmates.

•   Talk to owners of other types of pets—cats, fish, ferrets, or hamsters. Write a short paper comparing the care of these animals to the care of dogs.

•   Go to the library. Research the American Society for the Prevention of Cruelty to Animals, the American Humane Association, or the Humane Society of the United States. Report your findings to the class.

•   PETA is a Washington, D.C.-based organization promoting animal rights and the ethical treatment of animals. Do you think that animals have rights? Do animals in your country have rights? As a class, discuss this topic.

•   Go to a pet shop. Check the prices of animals. Look at the cages, food, and water of the animals. Compare the pet shop to a pet shop in your own country. Write a short paper on this topic.

•   Dogs star in many American movies, T.V. shows, and cartoons. Watch a movie starring a dog: *Lassie, Benji, Beethoven, Rin Tin Tin, Old Yeller, 101 Dalmations, Lady and the Tramp,* any "Peanuts" movie, or *Homeward Bound.* (Many of these can be rented at a video rental store or at a library.) Tell your class about the movie and about the dog's "personality."

•   Choose five to ten words from this chapter that are new for you. Write the words and write your own sentences using these words.

GLOSSARY

beetle, noun	An insect with a pair of hard wings.
behave, verb	To act appropriately.
obedience, noun	Doing what you are told.
shelter, noun	Protection.

E

Edible Things

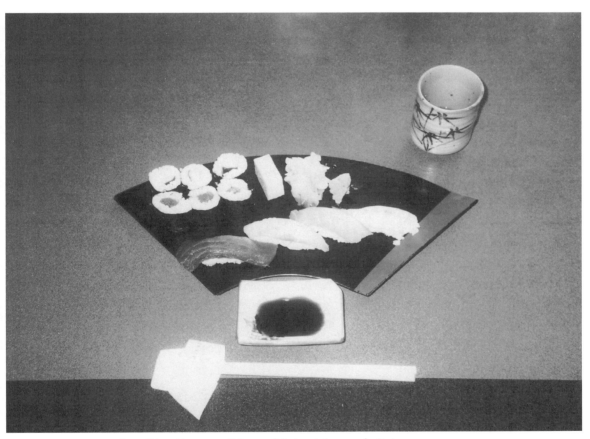

A traditional Japanese dish, raw fish, is gaining popularity in other countries.

Prep & Preview
· · · · · · · · · · · · · · · · · ·

Find the addresses of two or three nearby ethnic food stores. If there aren't any, find a supermarket with a good ethnic food section or try to locate ethnic restaurants or shops that sell some imported food items. You will go to one store.
Cost: $1.00–$5.00.

Before the Activity
· · · · · · · · · · · · · · · · · · · ·

1. Think about the foods you eat in your country. Are there any foods in your country that are not eaten in other countries? If you don't know any, talk to an American or a student from a different country. Write down the foods.

   _____

   _____

CULTURE NUGGET Humans eat almost anything you can think of, from the red thing on the head of a rooster to grasshoppers, puppies, and kittens. For the Aztecs, slime from the surface of rivers and lakes was a special treat. In the Rocky Mountain states, calf **testicle**s are considered a delicacy. According to psychologist Paul Rozin, the foods that disgust are almost all animal products, and people's tastes depend on their cultural background. (Eric Asimov, "Close Your Eyes. Hold Your Nose. It's Dinner Time," *New York Times,* 14 September 1997, section 4 page 2.)

2. Are there any American foods, or foods from other countries, that you consider strange and wouldn't be eaten in your country? If so, why?

   _____

   _____

3. Look at this list of foods, then complete the chart. Work in pairs. Discuss these foods. (You might need to use a dictionary or ask your teacher to explain words that you don't know.) If you have seen the food in the United States or in your country, put a check mark in the appropriate column. If you would be willing to try this food, put another check mark. If it exists in a classmate's country, put a check mark in the last column.

Digestible or Delectable?

Food	Example Country Where Food Is Found	Seen/Eaten In the U.S.?	Seen/Eaten in Your Country?	Would You Try It?	Seen/Eaten in Classmates' Countries?
bacteria	Lebanon				
blood	England				
bark	Mexico				
bamboo	Burma				
cat	Vietnam				
chicken bone cartilage	Moldova				
cow tongue	Mexico				
dog meat	Taiwan				
eye balls	Iran				
flowers	Cambodia				
fungus	Hong Kong				
horse meat	Ukraine				
insects	Taiwan				
jelly fish	Korea				
lime peels	Moldova				
mold	France				
monkey meat	China				
mushrooms	Russia				
octopus	Japan				
oysters	U.S.				
pig meat	Germany				
pigeon	Hong Kong				
pine cones	Turkey				
rabbit	Vietnam				
rat meat	Taiwan				
raw fish	Cambodia				
raw meat	Japan				
seaweed	Burma				
snails	France				
squid	Korea				

4. As a class, discuss your answers. For each item given, find out if it exists in a classmate's country. Write the name of the classmate's country.

    _____

    _____

The Activity

· · · · · · · · · · · · ·

1. Look in the phone book to find an ethnic food store that you could go to.

2. Call the store to check the hours that the store is open.

3. Name of store _____

4. Food type (country) _____

5. Address _____

6. Hours _____

7. Go to the store. Look around.

8. Date _____

9. Write down the names of three foods in the store that you've never seen before.

    _____

    _____

    _____

10. Buy something that you have never eaten before, and eat it. If it requires preparation, ask somebody who works at the store how to prepare or how to eat it. If that person has an accent or speaks too fast, ask him or her to speak slowly and to repeat the information. Write down the explanation he or she gives you.

_____

_____

_____

11. Name of food that you bought _____

12. Price _____

13. Describe the food. What did it look like? Taste like? Feel like? Smell like? Did you like it? Why or why not?

_____

_____

_____

14. Do you think that that food could become popular in your country? Why or why not?

_____

_____

15. Save the package from the food you bought. Staple it to this page.

After the Activity

. . . .

1. In the food chart that you filled out, did you say that you would try **fungus?** What about **mold?**

   _____

2. Many people eat fungus and mold, but they don't realize it. For example, mushrooms are a type of fungus. So is yeast, which is in bread and beer. Some cheeses, like brie, have mold on them. Yogurt contains **bacteria.** Have you eaten any of these things?

   _____

3. Think about how some words affect our views, and maybe even our eating choices.

   _____

   _____

4. Do you think that a tomato is a fruit or a vegetable? What about an avocado?

   _____

5. What's the difference between a fruit and a vegetable? Look them up in the dictionary.

   _____

6. Knowing this, do you feel different about tomatoes or avocados? _____

   _____

CULTURE

NUGGET

Some foods that might seem truly "American," aren't. The ancient Greeks chewed chewing gum. A Brit, Joseph Priestley, discovered carbonated water, which is used in soda pop. Ketchup comes from the Orient. Even ice cream goes back at least to the Roman Emperor Nero. What about pizza? And hamburgers? Do you know? Is there really any food that we can call "American?" (Rhoda and Leda Blumberg, *The Simon & Schuster Book of Facts & Fallacies* New York: Simon & Schuster, 1983.)

7.   Write down three new words that you used during this activity. _____

     _____

8.   As a class, discuss your experiences in an **ethnic** food store. Tell your
     classmates about the food that you ate.

9.   Talk about this activity with an American. Discuss the food chart you filled
     out.

Optional Activities
. . . .

•   Buy enough of your new ethnic food to bring to class. Let everyone try it.
    Talk about it.

•   Discuss some special foods or dishes from your country. Tell the class about
    them.

•   Prepare a special food from your country for your classmates. Have a **buffet**
    lunch or a picnic.

•   In America, there are lots of ethnic restaurants with inexpensive food. Go to
    a restaurant that serves a type of food you've never tried. Write or tell about
    the food that you eat there.

•   Get a recipe from a classmate for a food from his or her country. Prepare it.

•   Ask an American if he or she knows any uniquely American foods. Ask him or
    her where to buy it or how to prepare it. Try it.

•   Choose five to ten words from this chapter that are new for you. Write the
    words and write your own sentences using these words.

GLOSSARY

bacteria, noun	Microscopic organisms that live all around you.
buffet, adj., noun	A meal in which people serve themselves.
ethnic, adj.	To do with sharing the same culture.
fungus, noun	A type of plant that has no leaves, roots, or flowers.
mold, noun	A fungus that grows on old food or damp surfaces.
testicle, noun	The oval sex gland in the male.

F

Fahrenheit

If water is 212° Fahrenheit, can you put your hand in it?

Prep & Preview
· · · · · · · · · · · · · · ·

You will try to get a sense of Fahrenheit degrees through several short research steps and activities. You will also try to understand Americans' discomfort with the metric system.
Cost: Free!

Before the Activity
· · · · · · · · · · · · · · · · · · ·

1. How many degrees (Fahrenheit) do you think it is in your classroom, right now? (Do not look at a wall **thermometer** yet. Just guess.) _____

2. How did you make your guess? _____

3. Ask three classmates what they guessed in question 1. _____ _____ _____

4. If there's a thermometer on the wall, check it. If not, ask your teacher to guess the temperature. _____

5. Guess your body temperature (in Fahrenheit). _____

6. Guess the temperature outside right now. _____

7. Guess the temperature for freezing (water). _____

8. As a class, ask your teacher his or her answers to 5 through 7. Write down the teacher's answers next to your own.

9. Have you ever used Fahrenheit? _____

10. Do you think that most Americans can understand Celsius degrees? _____

11.   Why or why not? _____

_____

CULTURE   The Fahrenheit thermometric scale was created by German
NUGGET   **physicist** Gabriel Daniel Fahrenheit (1686–1736). He set the zero
               point of the scale as the coldest temperature for a water-ice-salt
               mixture. The second fixed point for the scale was the temperature
               of the human body. On this scale, then, the freezing point of pure
               water was 32°, and the boiling point of pure water was 212°. Most
               English-speaking countries used this scale until recently. Now, the
               Fahrenheit scale is being replaced by the Celsius scale.

12.   Read through the activity that follows. Make sure that you understand it.
      You may work with a classmate, or ask your teacher if you have questions.

The Activity

. . . .

1.   Ask a few Americans to guess the temperature outside. Write down their
     guesses to, "What do you think the temperature is today?" Then, ask them
     to guess the temperature in Celsius.

     Fahrenheit   Guess 1 _____   Guess 2 _____   Guess 3 _____
     Celsius   Guess 1 _____   Guess 2 _____   Guess 3 _____

2.   Ask a few more Americans at a different time and, ideally, a different
     temperature.

     Fahrenheit   Guess 1 _____   Guess 2 _____   Guess 3 _____
     Celsius   Guess 1 _____   Guess 2 _____   Guess 3 _____

3.   Look in a refrigerator. Find the temperature control button. What is the

     temperature **span?** _____

4.   Look on a milk carton. Is there a recommended temperature for

     storage? _____

5. Find the weather section in the newspaper. Check the temperatures in five world cities and write them in Fahrenheit. Staple the newspaper weather section below.

   _____   _____   _____   _____   _____

6. Watch the news on TV. During the weather portion of the news, the newscaster will tell you the exact temperature outside. Write it down.

   _____ Go outside and see what that temperature feels like.

7. Find a thermometer for taking human temperatures. What is the **range** of temperatures available? _____

8. Ask two Americans what their temperatures were when they were very sick.

   _____   _____

9. When you were sick, what was your highest temperature, in Celsius?

   _____

10. Look in a cookbook. Find a recipe for cake, bread, or pie. What temperature should you set the oven? _____ How much do you think this is in Celsius? _____

11. Look at an oven. What is the range of oven temperatures? _____

12. Look up "sun" in the encyclopedia. Find the sun's temperature. Write it down. _____

After the Activity

· ·

1. Try to make some good guesses at the temperature in Fahrenheit. (Do not calculate these. Just guess.) Try not to look at your notes from earlier sections in this unit.

    On a gray rainy day in October, what's the temperature? _____

    On a nice day at the beach, what's the temperature? _____

    On a deathly hot day in the Sahara desert, what's the temperature? _____

    When snow first falls in the winter, what's the temperature? _____

    What is your body temperature? _____

    What's the temperature outside today? _____

    What's the temperature in your house? _____

    If you bake fish in the oven, at what temperature might the oven be set?

    _____

    If you boil water, what temperature is the water when it boils? _____

    If a sick person has a dangerously high temperature, what might it be?

    _____

    If the date is July 3 in your country, what's the temperature? _____

2. In small groups, compare your answers with a classmate's. Discuss your answers.

3. As a class, ask your teacher what he or she thinks about your answers to the first question.

4.   Here is a method for converting Celsius to Fahrenheit.

To go from Celsius to Fahrenheit, multiply Celsius by 9/5, then add 32. For example, it is 14 degrees Celsius outside: $(14 \times 9/5) + 32 = 57°F$. So, it is 57 degrees Fahrenheit.

To go from Fahrenheit to Celsius, subtract 32 from Fahrenheit, then multiply Fahrenheit by 5/9. For example, you must bake a cake at 350 degrees Fahrenheit. $(350 - 32) \times 5/9 = 177°C$. So, you must bake the cake at 177 degrees Celsius.

5.   Do a few conversions from Celsius to Fahrenheit. You may need a calculator.

0°C = _____   0°F = _____

5°C = _____   30°F = _____

10°C = _____   50°F = _____

15°C = _____   70°F = _____

20°C = _____   100°F = _____

6.   Compare your answers with a classmate's.

Optional Activities
· ·

•   Check in the juvenile section in a public library for a science book, and read more about the creation of the Fahrenheit **scale** or about Gabriel Daniel Fahrenheit. Write a short report, and read it to your classmates.

•   Find a math book for grade school, middle school, or high school students. Look at the section on the metric system. Do you think it's useful for understanding the metric system?

•   If you were personally responsible for changing the U.S. measurement system to the metric system, how would you do it?

•   Interview a few Americans of different ages. Ask them when they first learned about the metric system. Ask them if they like the metric system. Ask them what they think about it. Write down their answers. Share their answers with your class.

- Choose five to ten words from this chapter that are new for you. Write the words and write your own sentences using these words.

GLOSSARY	
physicist, noun	An expert in the science dealing with the properties of matter and energy.
range, noun	The distance between two extreme points.
scale, noun	A device used to weigh something or someone.
span, noun	The distance between two points.
thermometer, noun	An instrument used to find the temperature.

G

Garage Sales

Clothes, toys, and decorations are among the common goodies at a garage sale.

Prep & Preview
. . . .

Bring a local weekend newspaper to class containing the ads for garage or yard sales. You will go to a garage or yard sale.

Cost: None—unless you buy something!

Before the Activity
. . . .

1. As a class, discuss garage sales. Does anybody know what a garage sale is? (If nobody knows, guess the meaning.) Write down your answer.

    _____

    _____

2. Confirm your answer to 1 with your teacher.

3. If you have been to a garage or yard sale, tell the class about your experience.

4. Are there garage or yard sales in your country? If so, tell the class about them.

5. How would you feel about buying used things from a stranger? Why would you feel that way? As a class, discuss these questions. Then, write down some of your ideas.

    _____

    _____

    _____

What are these men doing?

6. Look in the newspaper **classified** section. Find **advertisement**s for garage
    sales this weekend. Find a garage sale that you could go to. Paste the ad here,
    or copy all of the information.

7. Read through the activity that follows. Make sure that you understand it. You
    may work with a classmate or ask your teacher if you have questions.

The Activity

1. Go to at least one garage or yard sale. (You can go to the garage or yard
    sale from the advertisement you cut out. Or, if you drive or walk in any
    residential area on the weekend, chances are, you will find a garage or yard
    sale.)

2. Date _____

3. Write down four things that were being sold at the garage or yard sale. Write down the garage sale price, the **condition** (excellent, medium, poor), and **estimate** the price if the item were new.

Item	Price	Condition (excellent, medium, poor)	Estimated New Price
_____	_____	_____	_____
_____	_____	_____	_____
_____	_____	_____	_____
_____	_____	_____	_____

4. Write two things connected to the garage or yard sale that surprised you.

    _____

    _____

5. Were there things that made you laugh? If so, write them down.

    _____

    _____

6. How many people were at the garage sale (guess)? _____

7. Did you buy anything? If so, what? _____ How much was it? _____ Did you bargain on the price? _____ Have you used it? _____

8. If you buy something, ask the owner about it. Ask where he or she got it, and when. Write down the answer. (Be ready—he or she might give you a lot of information!)

    _____

    _____

    _____

    _____

9. Did you see anything at the garage sale from your country? If so, what?

    _____

    _____

10. How long did you stay at the garage sale? _____

11. Was it worth your time? _____

12. Optional: Take a photograph at the garage sale (ask the owner first). Paste it on this page.

13. Optional: Chat with the people who are holding the sale. Ask if it's their first garage sale. Ask them about something that they are selling. Ask if they've been busy.

After the Activity
. . . .

1. In small groups, or as a class, tell your classmates about your experience.

2. Have your feelings about garage sales changed? If so, explain how they have changed.

   _____

   _____

   _____

3. What would your mother say if you told her that you bought some dishes at a garage sale?

   _____

   _____

4. Would you go to another garage sale? Why or why not?

   _____

   _____

5. Would you hold a garage sale? Why or why not?

   _____

   _____

6. In your opinion, what are good things to buy at a garage sale?

   _____

   _____

   _____

7. What would you *never* buy at a garage sale? Why? _____

   _____

   _____

8. In small groups, discuss your answers to questions 2–7.

CULTURE NUGGET We aren't sure how garage sales began, but it's thought that they started because people in a wealthy society had lots of extra material goods. Rather than throw their goods away, people decided to sell them. Some think that garage sales have become popular in recent years because of the "nostalgia kick." (Jack and Chris Wilkie, *Trash and Treasure* [Tustin, CA: Bent Twig, 1987] and James Michael Ullman, *How to Hold a Garage Sale* [New York: The Benjamin Company, 1973].)

Optional Activities

- Go to a few more garage sales.

- Read the garage sale ads in the newspaper. What types of things are often sold at garage sales?

- Ask an American what he or she thinks of garage sales.

- Find an American who has held a garage sale. Talk to him or her about the experience. Write a report. Share it with your class.

- Hold a garage or yard sale. If you don't have enough things to sell, find some classmates or friends to help and to bring things to sell.

- Choose five to ten words from this chapter that are new for you. Write the words and write your own sentences using these words.

GLOSSARY	
advertisement, noun	A public notice that brings attention to something.
classified, adj.	Being grouped together according to characteristics.
condition, noun	The general state of something.
estimate, verb	To guess about an amount.

H

Holidays

This is an Easter basket. Where do you think these Easter eggs are from?

Photo by Craig Huber

Prep & Preview

You will learn about the major national U.S. holidays.
You might **celebrate** one holiday.
Cost: Free to cost of a party.

Before the Activity

1. What are the two biggest holidays in your country? In groups of three or four students, talk about the biggest holidays in your country.

2. What holidays do you know about in the United States? As a group, make a list of every U.S. holiday you know.

    _____   _____

    _____   _____

    _____   _____

    _____   _____

    _____   _____

CULTURE NUGGET   There are ten federal legal holidays in the United States. Government offices, including post offices and schools, are usually closed on federal holidays. However, there are several other popular holidays that are not federal holidays. For example, Valentine's Day and Secretaries Day are big days for celebration in the United States, but offices don't close because of them.

3. As a class, combine your lists. Write all the holidays on the chalkboard.

4. Ask your teacher to help you complete the list of common U.S. holidays.

5. As a class, talk about these holidays. What do you know? Which are religious? Which are federal holidays? How are they celebrated?

6. Work in pairs. Choose one holiday from the list above. Write down everything that you know about the holiday: its beginning, its history, its purpose, related customs, foods, colors, common forms of celebration.

_____

_____

_____

_____

_____

7. As a class, look on the next page at table 4, which is a list of federal and other popular holidays in the United States. Were there holidays that you had forgotten?

8. Work in pairs or small groups. Each group will choose one holiday from the list. You will research that holiday, become specialists, and make a presentation to the rest of the class. Look at the list and talk about which holidays interest you and which group you will be in.

9. As a class, decide which group will learn about which holiday. Try to cover all of the holidays.

10. Your group's holiday _____

11. Read through the activity that follows. Make sure you understand it. You may work with a classmate or ask your teacher if you have questions.

The Activity

· · · · · · · · · · · · ·

TABLE 4.   The Most Common Holidays in the United States

Holiday	Date Celebrated	Type of Holiday
New Year's Day	January 1	Federal
Martin Luther King, Jr., Day	Third Monday in January	Federal
St. Valentine's Day	February 14	Traditional
Presidents' Day	Third Monday in February	Federal
St. Patrick's Day	March 17	Traditional
All Fools' Day	April 1	Traditional
Easter	A first Sunday between March 22 and April 25	Religious
Memorial Day	May 26	Federal
Independence Day	July 4	Federal
Labor Day	First Monday in September	Federal
Columbus Day	Second Monday in October	Federal
Halloween	October 31	Traditional
Veterans Day	November 11	Federal
Thanksgiving	Fourth Thursday in November	Federal
Hanukkah	(Depends on Hebrew calendar)	Religious
Christmas	December 25	Federal, Religious, and Traditional
Kwanzaa	December 26 to January 1	Traditional and Cultural
Other holidays	You may know of other holidays that are celebrated in the United States. If so, you may want to study one of them.	

1.   Your group's holiday _____

2.   Research your holiday. You may go to the library. There are lots of great books on holidays in the children's and juvenile sections of the library. Also, you can read about holidays in the encyclopedia. You may also interview Americans to get information.

3. Choose at least two sources of information. Write them down here:

   _____   _____

4. Write down your information about the origins and development of the holidays.

   _____

   _____

   _____

   _____

   _____

5. Write down information about the purpose of your holiday.

   _____

   _____

   _____

   _____

   _____

6. Write down information about how Americans commonly celebrate this holiday. Include foods, colors, gift-giving practices, family gatherings, and so on. Also, write down who celebrates this holiday (not everybody celebrates the same holidays in the United States).

   _____

   _____

   _____

   _____

   _____

7. As a group, be prepared to tell your classmates what you learned.

8. Optional: Make a collage or a poster to represent your holiday. You may hang it in your classroom.

After the Activity

. . . .

1. As a group, present your findings to your class. Tell them everything you
    know about the holiday.

2. Listen to your classmates' information. Take notes about other U.S. holidays
    and write them below. If you don't understand, ask questions.

    New Year's Day

    Martin Luther King, Jr., Day

    St. Valentine's Day

    Presidents' Day

    St. Patrick's Day

    All Fools' Day

    Easter

    Memorial Day

    Independence Day

    Labor Day

    Columbus Day

Halloween

Veterans Day

Thanksgiving

Hanukkah

Christmas

Kwanzaa

Other Holidays

3. If you made a collage, hang it in your classroom.

4. As a class, talk about what you learned. Are U.S. holidays similar to holidays in your country? What holidays are they like?

5. Talk as a class, and with your teacher, about celebrating a holiday in your class. You may choose any holiday. However, it might be easier to celebrate a holiday if one is coming soon. If you choose to celebrate a holiday, you will need to think about several things: **decoration**s, educational films, food, guest lecturers, music, and so on.

Optional Activities
. . . .

*   Read and do research about another holiday.

*   Read more about your holiday.

*   If there is a holiday coming up soon, watch in the newspaper for community events related to the holiday. Attend an event. Take your camera! Be ready to report back to your class.

- Go to a greeting card store. Greeting cards are a common part of celebrating some holidays in the United States. Read a few cards. If you like one in particular, buy it and staple it to this page. (Or, mail it to a friend.)

- Rent a holiday movie. For example, *It's a Wonderful Life* is a Christmas classic. *Ghostbusters* is a Halloween movie. Watch the movie. How much of it can you understand?

- Choose five to ten words from this chapter that are new for you. Write the words and write your own sentences using these words.

GLOSSARY

celebrate, verb   To observe a holiday. To mark by engaging in a pleasurable activity.
decoration, noun   Something that is added to a place to make it prettier.

1

Indigenous People

A Native American family at the Colville Reservation in Washington State, sometime around 1900.

Special Collections Division, University of Washington Libraries, Photo by Edward H. Latham, Negative #1009

Prep & Preview

You will either visit a **Native** American museum , or you will go to the public library to research Native Americans.
Cost: Free—museum entrance fee

Note: This activity may be unpleasant for refugees of some countries.

Before the Activity

CULTURE NUGGET

When Christopher Columbus first arrived in America in 1492, he thought that he had sailed to India. So, when he saw the native American people, he thought they were the people of India and called them "Indians." Even though he was wrong, the name has stuck. These days, it is more common—and more correct—to call the indigenous people of America "Native Americans."

1. What images do you have of Native American people? Write down four or five words that describe your image of Native Americans.

    _____

    _____

2. Where did you get your image? _____

    _____

3. It is likely that just three hundred years ago, Native Americans lived on the land where your school now sits. Is there any evidence of that **civilization?** If so, what evidence is there?

    _____

    _____

4. If there is no evidence, why do you think there isn't?

    _____

    _____

    _____

 CULTURE **NUGGET** When Europeans first arrived in America, there were about 5 million Native Americans living on the land of the current United States. Today, there are about 1.4 million. (Anthony DePalma, "Three Countries Face Their Indians," *New York Times*, 15 December 1996, E3.)

5. In your country, was or is there an **indigenous** people and culture that was or is largely being destroyed by another people? Write about them.

    _____

    _____

    _____

    _____

6. Can you think of other countries in this century in which indigenous people/cultures have been pushed out by invading people?

    _____

    _____

7. There are many different, separate groups of Native Americans, called **tribe**s, including the Mohicans and the Cherokees. Can you think of other tribe names? Write down as many as you can think of. Where have you heard these names?

    _____

    _____

8. In pairs, share your answers to questions 1 through 7.

9. As a class, write down all of the names of Native American tribes that you thought of for question 7 above.

10. Read through the activity that follows. Make sure that you understand it. You may work with a classmate or ask your teacher if you have questions.

Native American carving

The Activity

. . . .

It is recommended that half of the class do Option 1 and the other half do Option 2. Some students may choose to do both, which is fine. After the activity, put all of your information together.

Option 1

. . . . .

1. Go to a public or school library. You may want to go to the juvenile or children's sections because there are many wonderful books in these sections about Native Americans. They are not difficult to read, and they have informative photographs.

2. Check out one book. (If you don't have a library card, you will need to get one. Bring your I.D. to the library with you. If you aren't eligible for a card, you will have to read your book in the library.)

3. Name and author of book _____

4. Read the book. It is not necessary for you to understand every word. It is only important that you get the main ideas.

5. Write down five new things you learned about Native-American culture or people.

    _____

    _____

    _____

    _____

    _____

6. Write down two things that surprised you, and write down why.

    _____

    _____

7. Write a one-page report about your book. Include the title and author of the book. Staple it to this page.

Option 2
· · · · ·

1. Using the telephone book or a local newspaper, find a museum of local Native-American art, history, or culture. Call the museum to find out the hours and costs. Write down the name of the museum, phone number, and hours.

    Name of museum _____

    Phone _____

    Address _____

    Hours _____

2. Go to the museum.

3. Date _____

4. Write down the names of tribes of Native Americans that lived in your part
    of the country.

    _____

    _____

    _____

5. Write down two things that you learned at the museum.

    _____

    _____

    _____

    _____

6. Draw a picture of a tool, piece of jewelry, piece of clothing, piece of art, or
    other Native-American **artifact** you observed. Describe it.

7. Write down two more things you want to know about Native-American
    people.

    _____

    _____

8. Go to the gift shop of the museum. They may have postcards or brochures.
    Choose something that will remind you of your day in the museum. Buy it if
    you want.

After the Activity

1. As a class, or in large groups, tell your classmates about your experience.

2. If you wrote a book report, read it to the class. Be prepared to answer
    questions.

3. If you went to a museum, bring the postcard or item you bought to class. Talk about your experience. Show your item to the class.

4. Listen to your classmates' information. Write down one thing you learned from each student.

   _____

   _____

   _____

   _____

   _____

5. As a class, think about the issues of human rights and peaceful coexistence among people of differing cultures. What international or national organizations exist that defend the rights of people? Make a list. Locally, how can you participate in the defense of human rights and the celebration of human diversity?

   _____

   _____

   _____

6. Has your view of Native Americans changed during this activity? If so, how?

   _____

   _____

   _____

   _____

   _____

Optional Activities

- Do the activity (option 1 or option 2) that you didn't do the first time.

- Read more books about Native Americans. Write another report.

- Go to another museum that exhibits Native American artifacts and art.

- If there is an Indian reservation near your area, go visit.

- See an old "cowboys-and-Indians" movie. For example, *How the West Was Won, The Searchers,* and *Wagon Master* are classics. What image of Native Americans does the movie give? Does this image match the information you researched? Why or why not?

- Ask an American about his or her view of Native Americans.

- Think about a people in the world whose homeland is being taken over by another people. Read about their situation in the newspaper or in the library. Compare their situation to that of Native Americans. Write a paper.

- Choose five to ten words from this chapter that are new for you. Write the words and write your own sentences using these words.

GLOSSARY

artifact, noun   An object made by human beings.
civilization, noun   A developed and organized society.
indigenous, adj.   Existing or produced in a region.
native, adj., noun Someone who is born in a certain place.
tribe, noun   A group of people who share the same customs and laws.

J
Jobs

Delivery person at work

Prep & Preview
· · · · · · · · · · · · · · · ·

You will learn more about jobs, especially jobs in the United States. You will interview an American, and possibly a classmate, about jobs.
Cost: Free!

Note: This activity is most appropriate for high-intermediate to advanced speakers of English.

Before the Activity
· · · · · · · · · · · · · · · · · · · ·

1. Think about a favorite job you have had. (It does not need to have been a paid job.) What were your **responsibilities?** Why did you like it? What hours did you typically work?

   _____

   _____

   _____

2. Think about the least favorite job you have had. What were your responsibilities? Why didn't you like it? What were your hours?

   _____

   _____

   _____

3. What is your "dream job"? Why?

   _____

   _____

   _____

CULTURE NUGGET The **federal minimum wage** in the United States, as of September 1997, is five dollars and fifteen cents. Minimum wage was first enacted in 1938 to protect workers by setting a minimum on their pay.

4. In groups of three or four students, talk about jobs that you have had. Tell your group about your favorite job, your least favorite job, and your dream job.

5. Do you have a job in the United States now, or have you ever had a job in the United States? If so, tell your group about the job(s). How is working in the United States different from working in your country? As a group, make a list of some differences.

    _____

    _____

    _____

6. Work together as a class. Students should write their dream jobs on the chalkboard.

7. As a class, think about each dream job individually. Brainstorm. Who do you know who already works in that dream job? What companies would have such a job position? Who works in a related field? Choose a class note taker to write down all of the ideas that you have for each job. Be specific.

8. Copy the list of names and companies that your classmates come up with for your dream job.

    _____

    _____

    _____

9. If two or three students have the same dream job, they may want to work together on this project.

10. Try to contact and interview a worker in the United States who has your dream job. Go to the activity that follows. Read it through, and write your interview questions.

Police officer at work

The Activity

1. From the list generated in class, from your personal contacts, or through the telephone book, try to contact a person who has your dream job. If you can't find someone with your dream job, find someone with a similar job. Tell him or her that you would like to do a short, **informational** interview with him or her about the job. Tell him or her that this is part of a class project and also a part of your career interest. Tell him or her that it will only take about 20 minutes. You may want to write a letter first. Then, you can follow up with a telephone call. If the first person you contact is not available, try again.

    In the United States, informational interviews are often done at the workplace of the interviewee or in a coffee shop. Ask the interviewee what would work best for him or her.

2. Who will you interview? _____ Phone number _____

    Company name _____ Date of interview _____

Time _____ Place _____

Classmates' names (if you are working in groups) _____

_____

3. Write your interview questions. The first ones are written for you.

Q: What is your job **title,** and what are your main responsibilities?

A: _____

_____

_____

_____

Q: What is your favorite part of this job?

A: _____

_____

_____

_____

Q: What jobs have you held in the past, or what experiences have you had
in the past, that taught you the **skill**s needed for this job?

A: _____

_____

_____

_____

Q: _____

A: _____

_____

_____

_____

Q: _____

A: _____

_____

_____

_____

_____

Q: _____

A: _____

_____

_____

_____

_____

Q: _____

A: _____

_____

_____

_____

_____

Q: _____

A: _____

_____

_____

_____

_____

Q: _____

A: _____

_____

_____

_____

_____

4. Ask a classmate, a native speaker, and/or your teacher to look at your questions. The contents of each question should be very clear.

5. Go to your interview. Ask your questions. Take notes about the answers. You do not need to write down every word. You can just take short notes. You might want to take your notes in your first language if this is more comfortable for you.

6. As soon as possible after your interview, type a one-page report about your interview (in English). Include the information you learned from the interviewee.

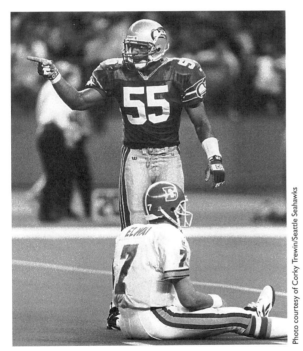

Photo courtesy of Corky Trewin/Seattle Seahawks

Football players at work

After the Activity

1. In large groups, share information about your interviews.

2.   Write down a summary of two or three classmates' experiences.

_____

_____

_____

_____

_____

_____

_____

_____

3.   If one of your classmates had an especially interesting interview, ask if you may copy his or her one-page report. Keep it in this book.

4.   As a class, think about writing thank-you notes. Your teacher can help you. Write a thank-you note to the person whom you interviewed.

5.   If you can, type the thank-you note. Send it.

Official U.S. Navy Photo by PHCS Ron Bayles

Mechanics at work

Optional Activities

- Find out if anyone in your class has held your dream job or a job that is related to your dream job. If so, interview that person about the job. Type a report about that interview, too.

- Arrange another interview in the community with someone else who holds your dream job.

- Go to the library. Read about the job field that interests you.

- Look in the newspaper job ads. See if there are many openings in the field that interests you. Cut out relevant ads. Tape them to this page.

- If you can work legally in the United States, apply for a suitable job that might lead to your dream job.

- Think of an appropriate **volunteer** position that you could do now that might give you some of the skills that you would need to get your dream job.

- Choose five to ten words from this chapter that are new for you. Write the words and write your own sentences using these words.

GLOSSARY	
federal, adj.	Having to do with a central government.
informational, adj.	Having to do with facts or knowledge.
minimum, noun	The littlest possible.
responsibility, noun	A duty or a job.
skill, noun	The ability to do something.
title, noun	The name of something.
volunteer, noun	A person who does work for free.
wage, noun	The money given for work.

K

Kissing

Who's kissing whom?

Photo by Robert West

Prep & Preview
· · · · · · · · · · · · · · · ·
You will compare some kissing habits in your country and in the United States by observing kissing in public. Cost: Free!

Note: It is suggested that students participate in previewing and selecting activities on sensitive topics such as kissing.

Before the Activity
· · · · · · · · · · · · · · · · · · · ·

1. In large groups, discuss kissing in your country. First, think of greetings and other types of social kissing.

   • Do people hug or kiss when they greet each other?

   • If people kiss when they greet, what is their likely relationship?

   • Do men kiss each other?

   • Do children kiss each other?

   • If people don't kiss, how do they greet each other?

   • In what other social situations do people kiss?

2. Write down one thing you said about your country that seemed to interest other students.

   _____

3. Write down one thing you heard about another country that interested you.

   _____

4. In some countries, everybody kisses babies. What about in your country? Discuss customs for kissing other people's babies.

5. In your same groups, discuss how **romantic** kissing in public is viewed in your countries. Think about these questions.

   • Do people kiss in public in your country?

- Where might they kiss? On a bus? In a park? In a movie theater? On a street corner? In a store?

- Who would be likely to kiss in public? (What age groups?)

- If a very **conservative** person in your country saw kissing in public, what would he or she think?

- Would they say or do anything?

- Are there any laws in your country about kissing in public?

6. Write down one thing that you said, and one that you heard, on this topic.

   _____

   _____

7. What about holding hands? Discuss how holding hands in public is viewed in each other's countries. Think of the same questions as in question 5.

8. Write down one thing that you said, and one that you heard, on this topic.

   _____

   _____

9. What do you think about kissing or holding hands in public places? Write at least one paragraph on this topic.

   _____

   _____

   _____

   _____

   _____

10. Read the activity that follows. Make sure you understand it. You may work with a classmate, or ask your teacher if you have questions.

The Activity

1. As you are in public, watch for people who are kissing. (Remember—it's not polite to stare!) Walk down the street, into a store, by a park, or through a parking lot.

2. Write down what you saw. Be detailed. How old were the kissers? Why were they kissing (take a guess)? How long did they kiss? Where were they? What time was it? Were other people nearby? Were other people watching the kissers? Did the other people look irritated or **amuse**d? Uninterested?

   _____

   _____

   _____

   _____

   _____

3. Talk to an American about his or her view of kissing in public. What are his or her ideas? Write them down. (Give the approximate age and **gender** of the American. Remember, it's better not to ask strangers how old they are.)

   _____

   _____

   _____

   _____

4. Ask the American to think of other words that mean the same thing as "kissing," such as "smooch." Write down the new words.

   _____

   _____

5. How do you say "kiss" in your language? Write down all of the different ways that you can think of.

   _____

   _____

   _____

CULTURE An American man named Alfred E. Wolfram kissed 10,504 people in 8 hours at the Minnesota Renaissance Festival on August 19, 1995. (*Guinness Book of World Records,* [New York: Sterling **NUGGET** Publishing Company, 1997].)

After the Activity
· · · · · · · · · · · · · · · · · · ·

1. In small groups, tell your classmates about your observations.

2. Talk about your interviews with Americans from question 3 of the previous activity.

3. Talk about your new words for kissing from question 4 of the previous activity. Write down your classmates' new words.

    _____

    _____

    _____

4. Tell your classmates some words from your language. Are any of the words onomatopoeic—that is, do they sound like what they mean?

5. In many countries, holding hands and kissing in public are considered socially unacceptable activities. Why do you think this is so?

    _____

    _____

6. Can you draw any conclusions about kissing habits in America? If so, write them down.

    _____

    _____

    _____

Romance appears alive and well.

Optional Activities

• Watch for more people kissing in public. Keep a list of your observations.

• Watch TV. Watch for people kissing. Keep a list of kissing on TV. Compare it to kissing on TV in your country. Compare TV kissing to public kissing.

• Talk to a few more Americans about kissing in public. Talk to people from different age groups. Write down their thoughts. Compare their ideas.

• Rent the movie *From Here to Eternity*. Examine the famous kiss scene (it takes place on the beach). In old movies, kisses are often unnaturally **melodramatic.** Why do you think this is true?

• Choose five to ten words from this chapter that are new for you. Write the words and write your own sentences using these words.

GLOSSARY

amuse, verb   To entertain or make laugh.
conservative, adj.   Moderate or cautious.
gender, noun   The sex of something.
melodramatic, adj.   Sensational and extravagantly emotional.
romantic, adj.   To do with love.

L

The Local Connection

Local musicians draw a weekend crowd at Jones Beach in New York.

Photo by Joe Budne

Prep & Preview

You will talk to one or two local people to learn about your city/area.
Cost: Free!

Before the Activity

1. In groups of three or four, talk about your town or the part of the United States that you are now living in. Write down everything you know about the five categories below. For example: History—When was this city started? Why? Who were the first **settlers**? Who named the city? What major historical **events** affected the city?

History	Current Events	**Economy**
Tourist **Sites**	Local Hotspots	

2. As a class, put together all of the information generated in question 1. Have one or two students write everything on the chalkboard. Add the new items to your own list in 1. If students disagree on certain points, put a question mark (?) next to them.

3. As a class, plan this activity. First, each group should choose one of the categories in question 1. Each group should choose a different category. Write it down in question 4 below.

4. In your small group, look at all of your information. What new information do you need to complete your knowledge of this area? As a group, make at least four new questions that would complete your knowledge.

    Your category _____

    Your group's questions

    _____

    _____

    _____

    _____

5. Each student in your group will be responsible for finding a complete answer to one of the questions. Choose your individual question, and write it in question 1 in the activity that follows.

6. Write your group's questions on the chalkboard.

7. As a class, discuss your questions. You may change your questions or add new ones. Give suggestions to your classmates. Use their ideas.

8. As a class, talk about how you can find the answer to your questions. Your teacher may help you think of ideas. For example, you may talk to local people or read the newspaper. Write down five possible sources of information for this activity.

   Talk to local people

   Read the newspaper

   Go to the Visitor's Bureau

   _____

   _____

9. In addition to your main question, try to get more information about at least four of the other questions. These questions may be from any category. Or, you may create other questions about your local area that interest you. Write your questions in the section that follows.

10. Ask a classmate to review your questions for grammar, clarity, and content.

11. Read through the activity that follows. Make sure you understand it. You may work with a classmate, or ask your teacher if you have questions.

The Activity

. . . .

1. Write your questions below.

   a. Main question _____

   b. _____

   c. _____

   d. _____

   e. _____

2.   Get a complete, detailed, interesting answer to the first question you wrote (a. Main question). Write it here. Give the source(s) of your information.

_____

_____

_____

3.   Get information on the other questions. Write it here. Give your source(s).

_____

_____

_____

_____

_____

4.   If they are available, get brochures, business cards, or pictures of your topic. Staple them here. If they're interesting and free, get extras for your classmates.

5.   Read the answer to your main question carefully. Be prepared to present your information to your classmates. Your presentation should last two or three minutes.

After the Activity

. . . .

1.   Rejoin the small groups according to category—that is, everybody whose primary question was in the history category should sit together.

2.   Talk about your new information. Decide who should make the first presentation. Who should be second? Third? Rehearse your presentations.

3.   Make your presentations to your class.

4. As a class, listen to all of the other groups' presentations. Write down the main points of each presentation.

    Presentation Category: History   *Presenters (students' names):*

    Category: *Presenters:*

    Category: *Presenters:*

    Category: *Presenters:*

    Category: *Presenters:*

5. Share information with the presenters. If one group says that Marco's Pizza Parlor is the best local pizza restaurant, you may want to give another opinion.

 CULTURE NUGGET (Write your own Culture Nugget. Show it to a classmate. For example, in the Northwest, you might learn that the local software company, Microsoft, employs over 17 thousand workers. (*Standard & Poors* [New York: Standard & Poor, 1997].)

 CULTURE NUGGET

Optional Activities

• • • • • • • • • • • • • • • • • • • •

- Choose another category that interests you. Do more research. Write a report.

- Choose a local hotspot or tourist site that interests you. Go to it. Take pictures. Tell your classmates about your experience.

- As a class, plan a fieldtrip. Go somewhere where you can learn more about your community. For example, go to a museum. Take a tour of a local factory. Go to a tourist site. Visit City Hall or a local television station.

- As a class, publish a short booklet on your community. Include each of the five categories (history, tourist sites, current events, local hotspots, the economy). Add art to the book.

- Ask your questions that you compiled earlier to someone who has lived in the community for many years. Compare the answers you get with other information.

- Invite a speaker to your class from the local Convention and Visitor's Bureau.

- Choose five to ten words from this chapter that are new for you. Write the words and write your own sentences using these words.

GLOSSARY	
economy, noun	The way a country runs its trade and money.
event, noun	Something that happens.
settler, noun	A person who moves to a new place to live.
site, noun	A place.

M
Movies

Moviegoers wait in line.

Photo by Robert West

Prep & Preview

Bring a movie **review** to class. You can find reviews in the movie section of the newspaper, in magazines, and on the Internet. You will read the movie review. Also, you will choose a movie to see.

Cost: $6.00–$7.00. If students have access to a video player and a public library that rents videos, possibly free.

Before the Activity

1. What is your favorite American movie? _____

2. In small groups or pairs, talk about your favorite movie. Tell your classmates why you like it. Tell them a bit about the **plot.**

CULTURE NUGGET

The famous "Hollywood" sign on the hill was erected in 1923 and was declared a historic landmark in 1973. It has appeared in countless movies and television shows. The first motion picture made in Hollywood was D.W. Griffith's *In Old California*. It took two days to film and told the story of lovers. (*The Guinness Book of Movie Facts & Feats* [Middlesex: Guinness Publishing, 1988].)

3. In groups, talk about your overall view of American movies? How did you form your opinions?

4. Write down other students' views of American movies.

    _____

    _____

    _____

    _____

5. Before you came to the United States, did you watch many American movies? Which ones? What did you like and dislike about them?

6. Think of five famous movie stars. What kinds of movies are they in? (Action, comedy, drama, historical, romance?)

7. In a newspaper or magazine, or on the Internet, read a movie review. If possible, read a review of a movie that you want to see. Write a summary of the review. Write the name and date of the newspaper or magazine. Staple the review to this page.

_____

_____

_____

_____

8. In groups, tell each other about the movie review you read.

9. As a class, discuss movie **rating**s in the United States: G, PG, PG-13, R, and X. What do these ratings mean?

_____

_____

_____

The Activity

1. In a local newspaper, find the movie listings. Find a movie that interests you. Make sure the rating is appropriate for you.

2. Name of movie that you want to see _____

3. Name/address of theater _____

4. Call the theater to find out the times the movie is showing. Write the times.

_____

5. Go to the movie.

6. Date _____

7. Who were the main characters in the movie? _____

   _____

8. What stars played in the movie? _____

9. Write a brief summary of the plot. _____

   _____

   _____

   _____

10. How much of the language in the movie could you understand? Give a

   percentage. _____

11. Was this more or less than you expected?

   _____

12. Did this movie fit your image of American movies? Why or why not?

   _____

   _____

   _____

   _____

After the Activity

1. In small groups, tell your classmates about the movie you saw. Would you recommend that others see the movie? Why or why not?

2. Listen to your classmates describe the movies they saw. Write the names of the movies they saw and a few words about each movie.

   _____

   _____

   _____

   _____

3. Which movie would you want to see?

   _____

4. Using the reviews you read as a model, write your own review of your movie. Staple your review on this page.

Optional Activities
. . . .

- Read a review of the movie that you saw. (If you already read one review for that movie, read another.) Do you agree with the reviewer?

- See another movie, either in a theater or a rental, with the same actors. Compare their performances.

- Watch Siskel and Ebert movie reviews on TV. They are famous movie reviewers. They grade movies with a "thumbs up," meaning a "good movie," or a "thumbs down," for a movie that they don't like.

- Watch the same movie you watched in the activity section again. Try to understand more of the English this time.

- Talk with an American about the movie that you saw.

- Tell the class about your favorite movie from your country. Ask your teacher if there is time in class to watch a foreign film, based on your suggestions!

- Choose five to ten words from this chapter that are new for you. Write the words and write your own sentences using these words.

GLOSSARY

plot, noun   The main story of a movie, play, or book.
rating, noun   A judgment, or a particular position or rank.
review, noun   A piece of writing that offers an opinion about something.

N

Newspapers

Sunday morning newspaper readers in a coffee shop. To many people, Sundays aren't Sundays if you don't read the Sunday paper, which is much larger than daily papers.

Prep & Preview
· · · · · · · · · · · · · · · ·

You will buy and read an English-language newspaper. Also, one student from each country group in your class should bring a newspaper from his or her country, if possible.
Cost: 25 cents–$2.00 per student.

Note: This entire activity can be done in class.

Before the Activity
· ·

1. As a class, or in large groups, talk about newspapers. Think of the questions listed below. (You may choose one student to lead your discussion.)

    What newspapers have you read in the United States?

    Did you like them? Why, or why not?

    In your own country, how often do you read the newspaper?

    In your country, can you get a newspaper delivered directly to your home?

    How do you prefer to learn about news: the newspaper, radio, TV, or another way? Why?

2. In same-country groups (all the students from one country), choose one student who can bring a newspaper from *your* country to class.

The Activity
· · · · · · · · · · · · ·

1. Buy a newspaper in English.

2. How much did it cost? _____

3. Name of your newspaper _____

4. Date of paper _____

CULTURE NUGGET The newspapers in the United States with the biggest circulation are, in order, the *Wall Street Journal, USA Today, New York Times,* and *L.A. Times.* (*World Almanac and Book of Facts* [Mahwah, N.J.: World Almanac Books, 1997].)

5. Cut out the **index/contents** list (it is usually on the first page) and paste it here.

6. Find two words you don't know in the contents listing. Write them down here.

    _____

    _____

7. Go to those sections of the newspaper. Try to guess the meanings of those two words, based on the contents of the sections. Write the meanings in task 6.

8. Quickly look at the **headline**s of several articles. Find a headline that has at least one word you don't know. Paste it here.

9. Read the first paragraph of the article that goes with the headline from task 8. Paste it here.

10. Choose one article that interests you. Read it. Cut it out and paste or staple it here (you may need to fold it).

11. Write a summary of the article.

    _____

    _____

    _____

12. How many articles are there in your paper about other countries? _____

13. According to the newspaper, is it an international, national, or local newspaper?

    _____

14. Look for an article about your country. If there is one, read it. Write a summary.

    _____

    _____

    _____

After the Activity

1. In large groups, compare your definitions and vocabulary in task 6 in the previous activity. Get your teacher's help.

2. Look at the headlines that you cut out. Talk to your classmates. Try to guess at the meaning of the words you don't know. Reread the first paragraph. It may help.

3. Read your article summaries to your classmates.

4. Discuss any interesting news.

5. In same-country groups, show the class and your teacher a newspaper from your country. Tell them about the different sections. Translate some of the article headlines for them. Give some information about some of the pictures in the paper.

6. Write down two interesting things that you learned about another country's newspapers.

    _____

    _____

7. Write down two ways in which your U.S. or international paper is different from newspapers in your own country/language.

    _____

    _____

    _____

    _____

Optional Activities

- Choose one **current** news topic that interests you. Read all of the newspaper articles that you find on this topic for one week. Keep a list of new vocabulary that you learn.

- Choose one current news topic that interests you. Read all of the newspaper articles that you find on this topic for one week. At the end of the week, give a presentation to your class on the topic.

- Read one different newspaper every Sunday for a month. Choose a mix of local, national, and international papers. Decide which you like the most. Tell your classmates about your favorite paper, and why you like it.

- Talk to an American about how often he or she reads the newspaper. How much of the paper does he or she usually read? Which paper does he or she read? Write a report on your findings.

- Write a class newspaper. You could write articles in pairs. You might have articles on many different topics: a student's country, class news, teacher's profile, school news, upcoming **event**s, and so on. Take photographs. Print the paper. Distribute it.

• Choose five to ten words from this chapter that are new for you. Write the words and write your own sentences using these words.

GLOSSARY

contents, noun	The things inside something else.
current, adj.	Happening now.
event, noun	Something that happens.
headline, noun	The title of a newspaper article, usually in big letters.
index, noun	An alphabetical list that shows you where to find things in a book.

O

Older Adults

Jogging keeps you healthy and strong.

Prep & Preview
· · · · · · · · · · · · · · ·

You will think about **senior citizen**s in the United States and in your country. You will observe seniors in America.
Cost: Free!

Before the Activity
· · · · · · · · · · · · · · · · · · ·

1. Think about seniors, or older adults, in your country. Write down five ways that a person's age may affect his or her actions. For example, in many countries, senior citizens would never go to a disco, just because of their age. They might not swim, or wear blue jeans, for example, just because of their age. (This question is not about activities connected to health limitations of older people.)

   a. _____

   b. _____

   c. _____

   d. _____

   e. _____

2. When you are 70, is there anything that you will *not* do, just because of your age? If so, what is it, and why won't you do it? (Let's assume you're in good health.)

   _____

   _____

   _____

3. In your opinion, at what age does "old age" start?

   _____

4. In large groups, discuss your answers to questions 1–3.

CULTURE NUGGET In the United States, a common **retirement** age is 65. At age 65, retirement used to be mandatory in the U.S., but now there is no age limit for retirement. However, it is at 65 that people can receive their full social security benefits. What is the retirement age in your country?

5. In your group, do you know senior citizens in the U.S.? If so, have you seen anything in their lifestyles that you probably would not see in seniors' lifestyles in your country? Share your thoughts with your group.

The Activity

TABLE 5

Behavior	Your country?	The U.S./Where/When
Chewing gum		
Wearing blue jeans		
Riding a bicycle		
Wearing makeup		
Drinking Coke or any soda		
Playing baseball		
Jogging		
Fighting/yelling in public		
Wearing a miniskirt		
Speeding in a car		
Playing Frisbee, hacky sack, or other park sports		
Tanning at the beach		
Jaywalking		
Shouting at a ball game		
Holding hands in public		
Going on a date		

1. Read the list in table 5. Now think about the behavior in your country. In just one afternoon of your daily life in your country, do you think you could find a senior who was doing this activity? Write "yes" or "no" in the first column.

2. Spend an afternoon in public in your town. Notice seniors in action. Go shopping, take a walk in town, or go to a park so that you will encounter older adults in public. Try to find senior citizens doing the activities in Table 5. Write where you observed the behavior.

After the Activity
. . . .

1. In large groups, discuss the observations you made during this activity.

2. Are you surprised by any of these observations? If so, which ones, and why?

    _____

    _____

    _____

3. Read your list of five activities that senior citizens would not normally do in your country (in question 1 in the previous activity). Did you see seniors in the United States doing any of these activities? Which ones? How did you feel when you saw them?

    _____

    _____

    _____

4. When you are 70, is there anything that you will *not* do, just because of your age? If so, what is it, and why won't you do it? (Assume you're in good health.) (You already answered this question before, but answer it again here.)

    _____

    _____

    _____

5. In your opinion, at what age does "old age" start? _____

6. Read your answers to questions 2 and 3 in the first section of this chapter. Compare them to your answers to 4 and 5 in this section. Have your answers changed? If so, why?

_____

_____

7. As a class, discuss your answers to 4, 5, and 6.

8. Do you think older people are respected more or less in the United States than in your country?

Optional Activities

. . . .

- Plan a visit to a senior center in your community. They are listed in the phone book. Call in advance to plan your visit. Plan a presentation about your country. You may want to work with a classmate. Bring photographs or items from your country to tell the seniors about.

- Translate the list of activities in table 5 and send it to a senior in your country. Ask him or her if he or she thinks these activities are appropriate for seniors, and if not, why.

- Visit a senior center in the United States. Talk to some seniors. Ask them about some historical events that they have lived through.

- Ask Americans when they think "old age" starts. Compare their answer to yours.

- Choose five to ten words from this chapter that are new for you. Write the words and write your own sentences using these words.

GLOSSARY	
retirement, noun	The time in life when you have given up work, usually because of age.
senior citizen, noun	Someone who is 65 years or older.

P

Police

Officers in Seattle can be found on horseback and on bicycles, too.

Prep & Preview
· · · · · · · · · · · · · · · · ·

Ask your teacher to call the local police department at least three weeks before this activity and talk to one of these departments: **Crime** Prevention, Community Policing, or Community Services. Request that an officer come to your ESL class and make a presentation on safety.
Cost: Free to the cost of a postage stamp.

Note: This whole activity is done in class.

Before the Activity
· ·

1. Think about the image you have of police officers in your country and of police officers in the United States.

2. Look at the list of adjectives in table 6. Circle the words that describe police officers in your country. (If there are words you don't know, ask a classmate or your teacher or look them up in a dictionary.) (For now, don't write in the United States column.)

TABLE 6

Your Country	The United States
able	able
bribable (can be **bribe**d)	bribable
cute	cute
dangerous	dangerous
easy	easy
fearsome	fearsome
great	great
honest	honest
intelligent	intelligent
just (fair)	just
lazy	lazy

Your Country	The United States
mean	mean
nice	nice
open	open
personable (friendly)	personable
quick	quick
relaxed	relaxed
sweet	sweet
tough	tough
understanding	understanding
vulnerable (weak)	vulnerable
wild	wild
xenophobic	xenophobic
young	young
zealous	zealous

3. Look at the list again. Think of your image of police officers in the United States. Circle the words that you think describe officers in the United States.

4. In small groups, discuss your answers. Talk about police officers in your country.

5. Where did you get your images of U.S. police officers? Write down the two main sources. For example, books, television, movies, or personal experience.

    _____

    _____

6. Have you ever spoken to or dealt with an officer in the United States? If so, tell your class about your experience. (Optional)

7. Prepare three questions you would like to ask a police officer in the United States. Write them.

_____

_____

_____

8. As a class, write your questions on the chalkboard. Look at all of your questions. Each person should have at least two questions that are different from your classmates' questions. Compare your questions. If your questions are the same as somebody else's, try to think of a new question.

_____

9. If you notice grammar or wording mistakes in your questions or your classmates' questions, make suggestions and corrections. If you're not sure, ask your teacher.

10. Read through the activity that follows. Make sure you understand it. You may work with a classmate or ask your teacher if you have questions.

The Activity
• • • • • • • • • • • • •

CULTURE **NUGGET**   Every 52 hours a police officer dies in the United States. (Channel 5 Evening News, _NBC_, 9 May 1997.)

1. A police officer will visit your class. The officer will talk to you about safety. Be prepared to listen carefully and to take notes. Also, be prepared to ask the officer your questions. (If your question is answered by the officer during the talk, skip it or ask another.)

2. Date _____

3.　Officer's name _____

4.　What were the main ideas in the officer's talk?

5.　What were some interesting facts or details in the officer's talk?

6.　What interesting answers did the officer give to your questions?

7.　If the officer has safety information, brochures, or stickers, staple or paste them to this page.

New York City police officers discuss a parade.

After the Activity

• • • • • • • • • • • • • • • • • •

1. As a class, discuss what you learned.

2. As a class, compare your notes from the officer's lecture. Did you write
    down similar things? Did you write down different things?

3. Look again at table 6 and words associated with U.S. police officers. Put a
    box around words that describe U.S. officers. After the presentation from
    the police officer, did your image of U.S. police officers change? If so, how did
    it change? Write your impressions.

    _____

    _____

    _____

    _____

4. As a class, or individually, write thank-you notes to the police officer. (Your teacher can help you compose a thank-you note.) You might mention in your note some of the specific information that you learned from the officer.

5. If the police station is near your school, choose a couple of students to hand-deliver your letter(s). Otherwise, mail them.

Optional Activities

· Find a television show about police. Some popular ones include "NYPD Blue," "Hill Street Blues," or "COPS." Watch one of them. Write a summary of the show.

· Notice police in your neighborhood or city. What are they doing?

· Read the local newspaper. Find a few articles that relate to police. Read them.

· Would you want to be a police officer in the United States? In your own country? Why or why not? Write a paper about it. Discuss it with an American.

· Talk to a few Americans about their images of police officers. Show them the list in table 6. Ask them to circle words that describe U.S. police officers. Ask them to circle words they think describe police in your country. Talk about it.

· Choose five to ten words from this chapter that are new for you. Write the words and write your own sentences using these words.

GLOSSARY

bribe, verb   To offer someone a gift or money to get them to do something for you.
bribable, adj.   Can be bribed.
crime, noun   Something that is against the law.

Q

Quick Stuff

You can make copies here fast.

Prep & Preview
· · · · · · · · · · · · · · · · ·

You will go shopping at a central shopping area or mall in your area. You will also talk to some Americans. Cost: Free—Unless you buy!

Before the Activity
· · · · · · · · · · · · · · · · · · ·

1. Some people think that America is a quick-action, fast-service, high-stress, consumer-oriented country. After all, the world-famous fast-food giant, McDonald's, started in the United States. Overnight mail is becoming the norm. We have "instant" meals. Many Americans even shave or eat breakfast in the car on the way to work in the morning. In small groups, talk about fast food, fast mail, and fast mornings in your country.

CULTURE **NUGGET** McDonald's is the world's largest quick-service restaurant. On any given day, nearly 7% of the American population eats at McDonald's. Not only Americans like the quick service. Canada opened the first non-U.S. McDonald's in 1967. Other big McDonald's-lovers include Japan, West Germany, Great Britain, and Australia. (*International Directory of Company Histories,* vol. 2 [Chicago: St. James Press, 1990].)

2. Have you seen any unexpectedly quick services or activities in America? What were they?

    _____

    _____

3. Have you seen any drive-through coffee stands? _____

4. What do you think of them? _____

5. Have you seen any unexpectedly *slow* things in America? If so, what? _____

    _____

    _____

6. In your country, what things seem too slow? _____

    _____

7. In class, start the activity that follows. Do step 1–2.

Dinner is ready!

The Activity

. . . .

1. Let's compare **speediness** in your country and in the United States. When we compare, let's consider small, locally owned stores. (It is not very interesting to compare the huge corporate giants, like Fuji Film and McDonald's, whose service is **streamline**d all over the world.) Work in pairs or in small groups. Look at the list of services and activities in Table 7. Think of your own country. In the first column, write how long in seconds, minutes, hours, or days, it would take for you to receive this service or do this activity in your country. (For now, do not fill in the second column.)

TABLE 7

Service	Local Store in Your Country (estimated time)	In America (time and source)
Get a package weighed and buy its postage for mailing (includes wait in line)		
Send a letter to another city 100 miles from your town		
Have a shirt dry-cleaned		
Get a haircut		
Develop a role of film		
Wait for a police officer to write a speeding ticket		
Buy an airline ticket by phone (includes time on hold)		
Get a prescription filled at a pharmacy		
Set up a bank account		
Wait to see a doctor		
Eat a breakfast on a weekday		
Greet an old friend who you meet on the street		
Order a hamburger		
Wait for a bus		
Get a passport (from initial application to receipt)		

2. Go to a shopping center in your community that has different kinds of stores, and go to at least four businesses or call four businesses. Ask how long it would take to accomplish four of the activities listed in table 7. Write the length of time and the source of your information (name of the store) in the righthand column.

3. Do at least one of the listed activities. Time it carefully. Write how much time the activity took.

4. Watch an American do at least one of the activities. Time it. Write the time.

5. Talk to Americans who have done the activities remaining on the list in table 7. Ask for time estimates. Write the estimates in table 7 in the second column.

Dry cleaning in one day

After the Activity

. . . .

1. In small groups, discuss and compare your answers above.

2. For which activities do the Americans' time estimates vary from each other the most?

_____

_____

3. Were there any lengths of time that surprised you? Which, and why? _____

    _____

    _____

    _____

4. Are there services in your country that are performed more quickly than

    they are in America? _____

    _____

    _____

5. Are there services in your country that are performed more slowly than

    they are in America? _____

    _____

    _____

6. Is America quick, after all? _____

    _____

7. Is it always good to be quick? When? Why or why not? _____

    _____

    _____

8. As a class, discuss your answers for questions 2 to 7.

Optional Activities

- Talk to an American about the speed of life in America. Ask if he or she would
  prefer a faster or slower life. Ask why.

- Write down all the events in your typical day in America and in your own
  country. Estimate the amount of time it takes to do each thing. What do you
  spend most of your time doing? Do you find that you spend the most time
  doing things you enjoy or not?

- Talk to an American senior about the speed of life when he or she was growing up. What activities took him or her a long time then that now don't take long at all? Does he or she think a faster way of life is an improvement?

- Choose five to ten words from this chapter that are new for you. Write the words and write your own sentences using these words.

GLOSSARY

speediness, noun   The quality of being very fast.
streamline, verb   To make simpler or more efficient.

R

Restaurants

This Mexican restaurant is close to the border. It's not the Mexican border, though; it's the U.S.-Canadian border.

Prep & Preview
. . . .

You will go to a restaurant for a meal. Try a new restaurant and new foods.

Cost: Depends on the restaurant you choose: $5.00–$25.00.

Before the Activity
. . . .

1. How often do you go to a restaurant for a meal in the United States?

   _____

2. How often did you go to restaurants for meals in your country?

   _____

3. In small groups, talk about your answers to the first two questions.

CULTURE NUGGET The average American adult eats four meals per week in a restaurant. (National Restaurant Association, telephone interview by Donna Stafford, 18 March 1997, Washington D.C.)

4. In your groups, talk about your favorite restaurant in your country. Explain why you like it.

5. Talk about your favorite restaurant in the United States, and why?

6. Write your answer to question 5.

   _____

   _____

   _____

7. In your country, what **ethnic** foods are most popular? Why do you think
    they are popular?

    _____

    _____

    _____

8. Name an ethnic food that you have never tried but would like to try?

    _____

9. As a class, collect the names of several inexpensive restaurants near your
    school. Choose several ethnic restaurants and/or down-home American
    restaurants. (Do not choose restaurants that offer American/international
    foods that you can buy in your country, such as pizza or burgers.) You might
    choose from restaurants you know, using the telephone book or with your
    teacher's help. Write all the restaurant names and the type of food, if you
    know it, on the chalkboard.

10. In groups of two or three students, choose a restaurant that you would like
    to try. Try to group yourselves with classmates who have a different native
    language from yours. Each group of students should try a different
    restaurant.

11. Read through the activity that follows. Make sure that you understand it.
    You may work with a classmate or ask your teacher if you have questions.

The Activity
. . . .

1. Call the restaurant that your group will go to. Ask for the hours for lunch
    and dinner. Get the address. Ask if you need a reservation. Ask the price
    range for their lunches and dinners.

2. Restaurant name/type of food _____

3. Restaurant hours: Lunch _____ Dinner _____

4. Address _____

5. Reservations needed? _____

6. Price range _____

7. Go to the restaurant.

8. Date _____ Classmates' Names _____

9. Read the whole menu. Write down three words that you don't know.

    _____

    _____

    _____

10. Looking at the menu, try to figure out three **ingredient**s that are common in that type of food.

    _____

    _____

    _____

11. Order something that you have never had before. Ask the waiter or waitress what the ingredients are.

    Your dish(es) _____

    Ingredients _____

12. The price _____

13. If you have a camera, take a picture of your meal. Later, staple it to this page.

14. Eat your meal. Describe how it tastes. _____

_____

_____

_____

15. Does it resemble any dishes in your country? If so, which ones? _____

_____

_____

16. Did you like the meal? Why or why not? _____

_____

_____

17. Ask your server if you can have a menu, business card, or brochure. Staple it to this page.

After the Activity

1. In class, in your group, prepare a small talk about your experience.

2. Make a short presentation to your class. Tell them about your experience.

3. After all of the presentations are finished, talk to your classmates. Talk to someone whose restaurant sounded interesting. Learn two more things. Get the hours, address, and price range for meals. Look at the menu if the students have it with them.

4. Write one paragraph about your restaurant or something you learned from other students about their restaurants.

    _____

    _____

    _____

    _____

    _____

    _____

5. Ask your teacher about his or her favorite ethnic food. Listen to your teacher's presentation.

6. Write down two things that you learned about your teacher's favorite ethnic food.

    _____

    _____

Optional Activities

• Write a review of the restaurant that you went to.

• Read a review of the restaurant in a local newspaper or magazine.

• Go to a bookstore and find a cookbook from the country whose food you tried. Look at the pictures. Skim a few **recipe**s. Prepare one recipe.

• Go to another restaurant featuring food from a different part of the world. Compare the two.

- If there are students in your class from many countries, prepare a presentation to teach them about food in *your* country. Make the presentation.

- Going to a restaurant for breakfast is quite common in America. Try it.

- Choose five to ten words from this chapter that are new for you. Write the words and write your own sentences using these words.

GLOSSARY

ethnic, adj.	To do with sharing the same culture.
ingredient, noun	An item used in making something.
recipe, noun	Instructions and ingredients to make food.

S

Supermarkets

Help yourself at this supermarket bakery.

Prep & Preview

You will think about supermarkets and the U.S. diet.
You will go to a **grocery store** and do a few tasks.
Cost: Free!

Before the Activity

1. In groups of four or five students, talk about your experiences at American supermarkets. Talk about these questions.

    *   Have you ever been to a supermarket in the United States? If so, which one(s)?
    *   What was your impression?
    *   How are U.S. supermarkets different from supermarkets in your country?
    *   Did you see any foods in the U.S. supermarket that you don't have in your country?
    *   Do you notice a difference in flavor or quality of fruits and vegetables in the United States as compared to your country?
    *   Are foods in the United States packaged differently than in your country? If so, how?
    *   Has your diet changed much since you've come to the United States? If so, how?
    *   Have you ever had a meal in an American home? If so, what was it like?

2. Write your answers to two or three of the questions above.

    _____

    _____

    _____

    _____

    _____

3. In your country, how often do you go to a supermarket? _____

4. What are the most common things that you (or your parents or spouse)

    buy at the supermarket in your country? _____

5. Who shops for your family in your country? _____

6.   In many countries, fruit and vegetables, meat, and bread are sold in small specialty stores. In your country, are such stores common? Where do you buy most of your food?

_____

_____

7.   Have you gained or lost weight since you've come to the United States? If so, how many pounds (1 kilo = 2.2 pounds). _____ (optional)

8.   In one day in your own country, how many teaspoons of sugar do you think you eat?

_____

CULTURE   In the United States, the average person eats an average of one cup of sugar every day. (Elizabeth Somer, "Sweet Delusions: We've Cut Down on Fat, But We're Eating More Sugar Than Ever," *Shape*, **NUGGET**   August, 1993.)

9.   When you were a child, how many dinners per week were cooked and eaten in your home? _____

10.   Have you ever been on a weight-loss diet? If so, did it work? _____

11.   Read through the activity that follows. Make sure you understand it. You may work with a classmate, or ask your teacher if you have questions.

The Activity
· · · · · · · · · · · · ·

1.   This activity has two parts. First you will go to a grocery store and do several activities. Then, you will interview an American.

2.   Go to a grocery store.

3.   Name of store _____

4. Date _____

5. Look at the signs hanging over the **aisle**s. These signs show the foods in that aisle. Copy one or two aisle signs here:

_____   _____

_____   _____

_____   _____

_____   _____

6. Circle any words that you wrote that you don't know.

7. Walk down the aisle. Look at the products. Try to guess the meanings of the words you didn't know. Write them here.

_____

_____

_____

_____

_____

8. Go to the dairy section. How many different types of milk are there (for example, 1 percent fat, non-fat or skim, acidophilus)? List them:

_____

_____

_____

_____

9. In your country, how many types of milk are there? _____

10. Go to the **cereal** section. How many types of breakfast cereal are there?

_____

11. Go to the meat section. How much does ground beef cost per pound?

_____

12. Go to the produce (fruit and vegetables) section. Find a fruit or vegetable that isn't common in your country. What is it? _____ (Buy some if you want. Ask the grocer how to prepare it.)

13.   Check the price of apples. _____

      Price of potatoes _____

14.   On every packaged food item in the United States, the ingredients are listed, as required by the government. In the supermarket, find the foods in the list below. Read the ingredients. If the item contains sugar, circle "yes"; if not, circle "no." (Note: Many words refer to sugar: corn syrup, high fructose corn syrup.) If you think sugar is a necessary ingredient in that product, such as in cake or cookies, circle "necessary." If you think it isn't necessary, circle "not necessary."

Food	*Sugar Necessary?*	*Sugar Contained?*
bread	necessary/not necessary	yes/no
canned peaches	necessary/not necessary	yes/no
canned soup	necessary/not necessary	yes/no
frozen pizza	necessary/not necessary	yes/no
peanut butter	necessary/not necessary	yes/no
spaghetti sauce	necessary/not necessary	yes/no
pasta noodles	necessary/not necessary	yes/no
yogurt	necessary/not necessary	yes/no

15.   Find two packaged food items in the store that you have never seen before. Read the package labels. Try to guess what they are. Write down the name and brand of the foods.

      _____   _____

16.   If you have your camera, take a picture in the supermarket. Attach it to this page.

17.   Interview an American. You may choose a shopper at the supermarket. Explain to him or her that you are doing a class project. You may also choose an American whom you know. Ask these questions:

      How often do you go to the supermarket? _____

      What things do you commonly buy at the supermarket?

      _____

      Who usually shops for your household? _____

      How much sugar do you think you eat in one day? _____

How many dinners per week are cooked and eaten in your home?

_____

Why do you think there are so many different kinds of cold cereal in the

United States? _____

_____

Do you think that food in the United States is cheap or expensive?

_____

Have you ever been on a weight-loss diet? If so, did it work?

_____

What are the two foods in question 15? _____

_____

After the Activity
· · · · · · · · · · · · · · · · · · ·

1. In groups of three or four students, compare your information.

2. Write down a classmate's new words task 5 and their meanings from task 7.

    _____

    _____

3. Talk about your answers to all of the activity questions. What things
    surprised you?

4. Compare the answers to your interview questions.

5. Can you make any generalizations about Americans' supermarket or dietary
    habits?

Optional Activities

• • • • • • • • • • • • • • • • • •

- Many packaged food items in the United States have a free, 800-number on them. Call one of these numbers, and ask the company a question about the product, such as, "Do you have a free recipe book for your product?" or "Do you have a sugar-free version of your product?"

- Read packages on everything you eat. Think about your sugar intake.

- Collect package labels that are small. Paste several in this book. Find some new vocabulary words on the labels.

- Make a list of ten common foods in your country. Estimate the price of the food in your country (in U.S. dollars). Then, go to the store, and check the price in U.S. dollars. Compare the two. Tell your class about your findings.

- Try one new food every week for a month. Write down the type of food. Draw its picture. Describe the flavor, smell, and texture.

- In the Sunday newspaper, find coupons for a local supermarket. Read a few. Staple them to this page.

- Choose five to ten words from this chapter that are new for you. Write the words and write your own sentences using these words.

GLOSSARY

aisle, noun	The path that runs between two things.
cereal, noun	A breakfast food that is usually eaten in a bowl with milk.
grocery store, noun	A store selling food and household goods.

T

Television

Do you think parents should limit their children's TV viewing time?

Prep & Preview

· · · · · · · · · · · · · · ·

You will discuss American TV and watch TV shows to do research. Each student should bring to class the TV **section** of the local newspaper or a TV guide. Cost: 25–50 cents per student.

Before the Activity

· · · · · · · · · · · · · · · · · · · ·

1.   Work in small groups or pairs to answer and discuss these questions.

2.   What is your favorite television show in your country? _____

3.   Are there a lot of American TV shows in your country? _____

4.   What is your favorite show in the United States? _____

5.   What have you noticed about TV in the United States? List three things. In your group, compare and discuss your answers.

_____

_____

_____

6.   How much TV do you watch in one week? _____

CULTURE
NUGGET
The average adult in the United States watches 31.5 hours of TV each week. (Gale Research Incorporated, Detroit, 1994.)

7.   Do you think that adults in your country watch more or less TV, on average, than adults in the United States? _____

8.   What is a reasonable amount of time to watch TV, in your opinion?

_____

9.   In your groups, discuss your answers to questions 5 through 7.

10. Look at your TV schedule or TV guide. Staple the **schedule** here.

11. Find two shows that you'd like to watch. Circle them. Find a description of the shows. Read them. Tape them here.

12. Read the activity that follows. You will choose one of the activities, A, B, or C.

13. As a class, make sure that all of the activities (A, B, and C) will be done. That is, all students should not do the same activity.

14. Read through the activity that follows. Make sure you understand it. You may work with a classmate, or ask your teacher if you have questions.

The Activity

. . . .

As a class, you will do some informal television research. (All observation should come from general public television instead of cable.) Choose one of the activities below (A, B, or C).

Activity A

. . . .

1. Using a TV listing, choose any TV show that interests you. You will watch the show. Before you watch it, read the questions below. When you watch it, have a clock with a second hand, this book, and a pen with you.

2. Name of show _____

3. Day and listed time of show _____

4. Channel _____

5.   What time did the show actually start? _____

6.   How many commercial **break**s were there? _____

7.   How many total commercials were there? _____

8.   How many minutes of time did **commercial**s occupy? _____

9.   What time did the show actually end? _____

10.   Do some math. How long did the show itself actually run? _____

11.   Write a summary of the show and of your impressions.

_____

_____

_____

_____

_____

Activity B
· · · · · · ·

1.   Choose a television show that is a sitcom (situation-comedy). You will watch the show. Before you watch it, read the questions below. When you watch it, have a clock with a second hand, this book, and a pen with you.

2.   Name of show _____

3.   Day and time of show _____

4.   Channel _____

5.   How many characters were in the show? _____ Who were they? _____

_____

6.   How many separate scenes were there? _____

7.   Time a few scenes. How long were the scenes? _____

8.   Many U.S. TV sitcoms have "canned laughter." That means that taped laughter is played during the TV show after something funny happens.

Count the number of times that canned laughter is played. _____

9. Could you usually understand what was funny? _____

_____

10. Write a summary of the show and of your impressions.

_____

_____

_____

_____

_____

Activity C
· · · · · · ·

1. Choose a national newscast on ABC, NBC, or CBS. You will watch the show. Before you watch it, read the questions below. When you watch it, have a clock with a second hand, this book, and a pen with you.

2. Name of show _____

3. Day and time of show _____

4. Channel _____

5. What was the opening story? _____

_____

6. What was the most interesting story to you, and why?

_____

_____

_____

7. How many minutes of the show were spent on sports? _____

8. How many were spent on international news? _____

9. What was the least interesting story to you, and why?

_____

_____

_____

After the Activity
· · · · · · · · · · · · · · · · · · ·

1. Make small groups. Each group should have at least one student from each activity (A, B, or C).

2. Tell your group about your findings.

3. Listen to your classmates' findings.

4. Make new groups. Now all those who did activity A will work together; the same for B's and C's. Discuss your findings. Write a summary of your findings about American television.

_____

_____

_____

_____

_____

_____

5. Choose a spokesperson for your group. Present your findings to the class.

6. As a class, discuss your findings.

7. Talk about your impression of TV in your country. In what ways is it similar to TV in the United States? How is it dissimilar?

_____

_____

_____

_____

_____

Optional Activities

- Do the two activities that you didn't do the first time.

- Translate this activity and send it to a friend in your own country. Ask him or her to mail you the results. Share the information with your class.

- Watch a **serial** show or soap opera every day for one week (if it's daily) or one month (if it's weekly). See if you can understand more of the English over time.

- Create a list of your own questions about TV in America. Watch a couple of shows to gather answers to your questions. Share your information with the class.

- Find a show on public TV (television that is supported by public funding) that interests you. Watch it. Compare it to your commercial TV (TV supported by commercial advertisers) observations.

- Choose five to ten words from this chapter that are new for you. Write the words and write your own sentences using these words.

GLOSSARY	
break, noun	A pause or a rest.
commercial, noun	An advertisement.
schedule, noun	A plan or a timetable.
section, noun	A part of something.
serial, adj.	Presented or told in several parts.

U

Universities

Graduates wear a cap and gown at their graduation ceremony.

Prep & Preview

You will take a **campus** tour at a university. You will need some catalogs for a couple of local universities or colleges. If your ESL class is at a university or college, your school's catalog will work too. You will look at the catalog, plan, and take the campus tour. Cost: Free to catalog cost.

Before the Activity

CULTURE NUGGET

Of Americans who are 25 years and older, 23 percent have a **bachelor's degree** or higher. Of Americans who are 25 years and older, 18 percent don't have a high school **diploma.** (*World Almanac* [Mahwah, N.J.: World Almanac Books, 1997].)

1. In a small group, talk about your impressions of U.S. colleges or universities. If you are currently in a college or university, talk about your impressions of what it would be like before you came to the United States, and talk about your impressions now. Compare your impressions.

2. Write down five adjectives you think describe U.S. universities.

    _____

    _____

    _____

    _____

    _____

3. Look up the words "college" and "university" in a dictionary. What is the difference between the two?

    _____

    _____

4. In your group, look at the catalog for one university or college near your school. Answer these questions:

When was the school founded? _____

How many students does it have? _____

Does it offer **undergraduate, graduate,** or **doctoral degrees,** or all of

these? _____

_____

What is the **tuition** for one year (or one semester)? _____

Are ESL courses offered? _____

Are courses in your native language offered? _____

Is on-campus housing available? _____

Find a course that you are surprised to find in the catalog. What's its title?

_____

Why does it surprise you? _____

5. Change groups. Tell your new group about the school that you read about. Hear about the others' schools. Write down the names of the other colleges and some basic information about those schools.

_____

_____

_____

_____

_____

_____

6. Read about the activity that follows. Talk to classmates to see if you are interested in the same college.

7. Write your questions for task 9 in the following activity in the answer lines on page 148.

The Activity

. . . .

1. Choose one university or college near you that you will visit. You may choose the school from the catalog that you read, or you may choose a school that other students studied. Or, you may find another school in the phone book.

2. Name of university or college _____

3. What is the phone number for the Admissions Department? _____

4. What is the address of the school? _____

5. Call the school. Ask about campus tours. Choose a day to take a tour.

6. Tour day and time _____ Tour meeting place _____

   _____

7. Make plans for getting to the university. You may want to go with a classmate.

8. Before you take the tour, read through the questions below. Also, write four or more of your own questions.

9. Take the tour. Write your answers.

   a. Name of tour guide _____

   b. Number of people on the tour _____

   c. When was the school founded? _____

   d. How many students does it have? _____

   e. What is the school's biggest department? _____

   f. What is the tuition for one year (or one semester)? _____

   g. Are ESL courses offered? _____

   h. Is on-campus housing available? _____

   i. How much does on-campus housing cost? _____

   j. How do you apply to this college? _____

   k. Get a brochure, postcard, or application for this college. Staple it to this page. Write four questions of your own about the university.

l. _____

m. _____

n. _____

o. _____

During their school years, students have to hit the books if they want to graduate.

After the Activity

• • • • • • • • • • • • • • • • • •

1. Make a presentation to your class about your tour.

2. Let your classmates ask you questions. Try to answer.

3. In small groups, discuss your observations.

4. Write down five adjectives that describe the university you toured.

    _____

    _____

    _____

    _____

    _____

5. Look back to the five adjectives that you wrote in the first section of this chapter. Were any the same? If so, why? If not, what do you think?

    _____

    _____

    _____

6. In small groups or pairs, talk to other students about their experiences.

7. Talk about colleges and universities in your country. How are they similar to the university that you visited here? How are they different?

Optional Activities

•   Find the addresses of two colleges or universities that interest you but that aren't near your area. Write to the institutions. Ask for a catalog. Look at it.

•   Take a campus tour at a different college.

•   Try to find an American college student to talk to about college life.

•   If you were going to attend a college in the United States, what would you study, where would you study, and why? Write a paper. Talk about it with a classmate.

•   Find out what the GED is.

- In a local college admissions office, read about college tuition scholarships. Find two **scholarship**s that you qualify for.

- Choose five to ten words from this chapter that are new for you. Write the words and write your own sentences using these words.

GLOSSARY

bachelor's degree, noun	A college or university degree given for four-year's of study.
campus, noun	The grounds of a school or college.
degree, noun	A title given by a college or university.
diploma, noun	A certificate from school that shows completion.
doctoral, adj.	The highest degree given by universities.
graduate, noun	Someone who has completed school and received a diploma.
scholarship, noun	A grant that pays for your college or course of study.
tuition, noun	The charge for instruction.
undergraduate, noun	A student who has not yet received the bachelor's degree.

V

Volunteers

At the Next Step Learning Center in Oakland, California, a volunteer tutor helps a student prepare for the General Educational Development test.

Prep & Preview
· · · · · · · · · · · · · · ·

You will gather information about places where you can **volunteer** your help or meet **volunteer**s. Then, you will volunteer some time or interview another volunteer. You may need a telephone book.
Cost: One postage stamp.

Before the Activity
· · · · · · · · · · · · · · · · · · · ·

1. As a class, talk about volunteering. Do you know what it means? Look up the word "volunteer" in the dictionary or glossary. _____

    _____

    _____

2. Have you ever volunteered in your country? If so, when and where?

    _____

    _____

    _____

3. Do you know others who have volunteered in your country? If so, who was it and what work did they volunteer for? _____

    _____

    _____

    _____

4. In small groups, talk about your answers to questions 2 and 3.

CULTURE NUGGET   Forty-eight percent of American adults do volunteer work. (1994 Gallup Organization national survey, *Giving and Volunteering in the United States*, commissioned by INDEPENDENT SECTOR. In "Community: The Barn Raising Spirit Still Thrives" by Alan Bunce, *Christian Science Monitor* 88, no. 106 (April 26, 1996).

5. Look at this list of common areas in which Americans volunteer their time and energy.

animal care	hunger and homelessness
arts	**literacy**
children	nature and the environment
churches or other worship centers	politics and government
crises	prisons
diseases and disabilities	schools
drugs and alcohol	**social service** organizations
hospitals	sports organizations
retirement homes/the elderly	youth programs

6. If you were going to volunteer, which area would interest you? Circle two areas.

7. As a class, talk about places in your community that are likely to use volunteers. With your teacher's help, try to think of specific places. (Your own school may use volunteers for math or reading tutoring.) Write them on the chalkboard. Also, write them here.

_____

_____

_____

8. If your list generated by the class is limited, you might contact your local United Way for ideas. Also, several national organizations have local chapters that may need volunteers—for example, the Boys Clubs of America, Girl Scouts of America, National AIDS Network, National Easter Seal Society, and the Salvation Army. You will also find a Volunteers-Needed column in the classified section of the newspaper.

9. Read through the activity that follows. Note: There are two options to choose from in this chapter. Read both of the optional activities and choose one you would like to do.

The Activity
• • • • • • • • • • • •

1. From your class list, or from your own research, choose a place that interests you. Then read about the two options below. Choose the one that you like. You may want to work with a classmate.

2. Name of the organization _____

3. Phone number _____

4. Call the place from your class list and talk to the **coordinator** of volunteers or executive director. Tell the coordinator your name and your school. Tell him or her that you are doing a school project on volunteers.

5. Volunteer coordinator's name _____

Photo by Jan Bogle

Dorothy volunteers her time to Virginia Mason Hospital in Seattle, Washington.

Option 1

. . . . .

1. Ask the volunteer coordinator if the organization has any special projects that you could volunteer to do. Tell them honestly and openly how much time you are willing to work (two hours? two days? two weeks? two months?). Remember: Some organizations have long training programs for volunteers while others request a minimum time commitment.

2. If the coordinator agrees to use your volunteering, set up your work schedule.

   Write it here: _____

   _____

3. If you can't actually volunteer, ask if you can spend a few hours with another volunteer, just to watch.

4. Get the address and other relevant information (such as what to wear, or which is the volunteer coordinator's office).

   _____

   _____

5. Volunteer or observe. Go, according to your schedule, to the organization where you will work.

6. Write a full page about your volunteering (or observation) experience, including where you went, what you did, how you were trained, who you met, and what was or wasn't interesting to you. Also, explain how you felt during your experience. Attach your sheet to this page.

7. Be prepared to share your experience with your classmates.

Option 2

. . . . .

1. Ask the volunteer coordinator if they can help you set up an interview with one of the volunteers. The interview will take about 15 minutes. If the coordinator agrees, arrange a date and time for the interview. (The coordinator may need to call you back.)

2.   Date and time of interview _____

3.   If the interview isn't possible, thank the coordinator. Remember: Volunteers are busy people. Also, their organizations may have rules restricting interviews. Try calling one or two other places that use volunteers. (If you don't succeed, you may try another place. Or, perhaps you can join a classmate in an interview.)

4.   Prepare a list of interview questions below. Be sure to get the name of the person you interviewed, where that person works, and what tasks he or she does. You may ask about why he or she volunteers. How much time does he or she volunteer per week? For how many years has he or she volunteered? What does he or she like and dislike about the work? Also, think of your own questions.

_____

_____

_____

_____

_____

_____

_____

_____

_____

_____

_____

_____

_____

5.   Write a full-page summary of your interview. Attach the sheet to this page.

6.   Be prepared to share your experience with your class.

After the Activity

1. In small groups or as a class, share your experience. Be prepared to answer your classmates' questions.

2. Listen to your classmates' interesting experiences. Write two or three things that you learned or questions that you have.

    _____

    _____

    _____

3. As a class, discuss your experiences. Has your view of volunteering changed?

4. Based on everything you heard, if you were going to volunteer for a long time period, where would you want to volunteer, and why? Talk about it.

5. Write thank-you notes to the places that you visited. You may also choose to send a copy of the one-page summary that you wrote. Mail your note within one week of your visit.

Optional Activities

*   Do this activity again using another organization.

*   Read other classmates' full reports on their experience. If a particular report interests you, ask if you may copy it. Staple it to this page.

*   Continue to volunteer on a regular basis.

*   In your day-to-day life, if you meet people who you think are volunteers, ask them if they are volunteers. If they are, ask them about their work, their experience, how long they've volunteered, and if they enjoy it.

- Do the option in this activity that you didn't choose to do the first time.

- Choose five to ten words from this chapter that are new for you. Write the words and write your own sentences using these words.

GLOSSARY

coordinator, noun	A person who organizes activities.
literacy, noun	The quality of being able to read and write.
prison, noun	A building where people live as punishment for a crime.
social service, noun	Work done for society.
volunteer, noun, adj.	A person who does work for free; free work.

W

Wheelchairs

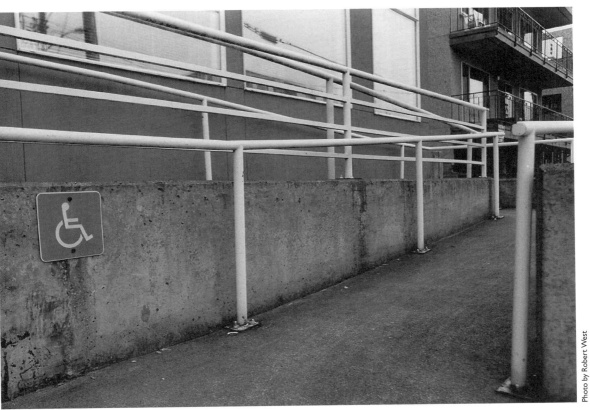

Photo by Robert West

Wheelchair ramps make many buildings accessible to wheelchair users.

Prep & Preview
· · · · · · · · · · · · · ·
You will think about wheelchairs and wheelchair users, and you will test your community for wheelchair **accessibility.**
Cost: Free!

Note: This activity was written for students who are *not* wheelchair users. Wheelchair users are encouraged to adapt this activity to their own experiences and knowledge.

Before the Activity
· ·

1. Do you know anybody who uses a wheelchair in your country? If so, write about some of the daily difficulties associated with the chair. If not, imagine yourself in a wheelchair. Think about your day, step by step, and about the difficulties you would face. For example, does the building you are now in, as you read this, have an elevator? Try to come up with four specific problems for wheelchair users that can be found in your country.

   _____

   _____

   _____

   _____

2. In groups of three or four, talk about your answers to the first question.

3. In your groups, think about your observations of wheelchairs in the United States. Have you seen any features in buildings, roads, sidewalks, restaurants, hotels, schools, or other public places that may have been designed specially for wheelchair users? If so, write them down.

   _____

   _____

   _____

CULTURE NUGGET According to the Americans with Disabilities Act, enacted in 1990, major public and commercial facilities in the United States must be accessible to disabled people. This means that elevators, ramps, telephones, bathrooms, drinking fountains, and telecommunications support (for deaf people) need to be available. The ADA also protects the **civil rights** of individuals with disabilities in the areas of employment and government services.

4. In your groups, think about your own countries and whether there are any special public **accommodation**s for wheelchair users or for people with other special physical limitations? Make a list.

    _____

    _____

    _____

5. As a class, put together your answers to questions 3 and 4. Write them on the chalkboard.

The Activity

. . . .

1. Alone or with a classmate, spend one or two hours in your community. Watch for specific accommodations that are provided for people with physical limitations of any sort. Write them here. Also, write where you saw them. Hint: Check parking lots, restaurants, public building entrances, banks, schools, libraries, buses, restrooms, and sidewalk curbs.

    _____

    _____

    _____

    _____

    _____

2.   If you see anybody using these accommodations, write down your observations.

_____

_____

_____

_____

_____

3.   During your outing, watch for signs, announcements, or literature about wheelchair accommodations. What words and symbols are used to indicate assistance for people with physical limitations? Find as many as you can. Write them down.

_____

_____

_____

_____

4.   Talk to an American. Ask him or her what other words are used to mean "disabled."

_____

_____

5.   In the phone book, find the name of a major hotel in your town. Call the hotel. Ask if rooms for wheelchair users are available.

Hotel name _____

Wheelchair-user rooms __Yes/No__

[Optional for advanced students: Ask what features the wheelchair room has.]

_____

_____

_____

After the Activity

. . . .

1. In large groups, or as a class, share your research with your classmates.

2. Make lists on the chalkboard of your observations to questions 1, 2, and 3.

3. Think about the word "disabled." What are the main parts of the word? Are wheelchair users really "disabled"? Are other people with physical limitations "disabled"? As a class, discuss your ideas.

4. What other words did Americans give you (question 4)? As a class, make a list on the chalkboard. Add your classmates' words to your list.

5. Which words do you like the best? Can you think of a better word? If so, write it down: _____ . As a class, discuss your ideas.

6. In your native language, what are the words for people who are disabled? Does your language have a better word than English?

7. Again, think of yourself in a wheelchair. Write down two accommodations that you have not already seen that you think might make your life easier. As a class, talk about your ideas.

_____

_____

Optional Activities

. . . .

•   Go to the library and read about the Americans with Disabilities Act.

•   If you know somebody who uses a wheelchair, show him or her this chapter. Chat with that person.

•   As a class, try to think of three famous people, past or present, who use(d) a wheelchair. Read about them in the library.

- If you were in a wheelchair, what activities would you no longer be able to do that you would miss the most?

- Choose five to ten words from this chapter that are new for you. Write the words and write your own sentences using these words.

GLOSSARY	
accessibility, noun	The quality of being easy to approach or enter.
accommodation, noun	Something given as a help or convenience.
civil rights, noun	Rights guaranteed by the Constitution of the United States and by other acts of Congress.

X

Xenophilia

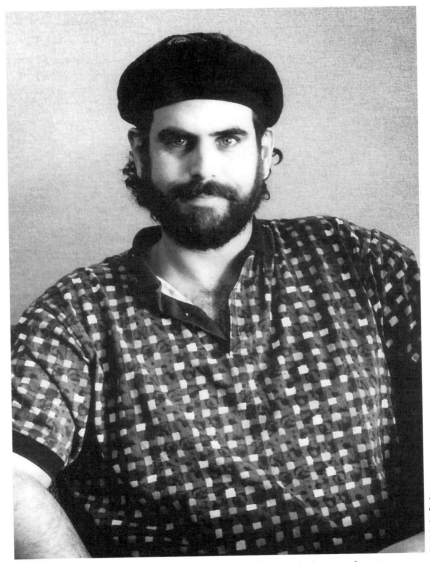

Photo by Jan Bogle

A second-generation Russian-American who eats Thai food whenever he gets the chance.

Prep & Preview
· · · · · · · · · · · · · · ·

You will interview an American, or another student, from a country other than your country, about his or her knowledge of your country. You will try to see how their knowledge of your country affects their attitude about it.
Cost: Free!

Before the Activity
· · · · · · · · · · · · · · · · ·

1. Look at this list of countries. Circle one country that you know almost nothing about.

    Burma   Papua New Guinea
    Canada   Czechoslovakia
    Egypt   Sri Lanka
    Finland   Tunisia
    Germany   Turkey
    Mexico

2. Write any impressions or ideas you have about that country, even if you are not sure they are correct.

    _____

    _____

    _____

3. Look at the list again. Circle a country that you are knowledgeable about. Write any impressions, ideas or facts you have about that country.

    _____

    _____

    _____

4. In small groups, talk about your answers to questions 2 and 3.

5. Based on your discussions, can you see any connection between one's knowledge about a country and one's impression? For example, if a person has little knowledge of a country, does he or she tend to have a favorable or a negative view of the country? As a group, discuss this topic. Write down some of your main ideas.

    _____

    _____

    _____

6. You will interview an American or another noncitizen of your country to find out what he or she knows about your native country and his or her opinions. Go to the activity that follows and read it. Write your interview questions.

This American woman loves African cotton fabrics.

Photo by Jan Bogle

The Activity

1. Write down ten or fifteen interview questions about your native country on the question list on page 169–71. Try to include questions on several different topics. For example, you might ask about **geography,** sports, language, politics, history, economics, religion, people, population, entertainment, education, or food. The first few questions are already written.

2. Ask the interview questions to an American. Write the American's answers on the answer lines.

3. After the interview, discuss your country with the person. Answer his or her questions. Look at an **atlas** or a map together. Help him or her to know more about your country.

Interview Questions

Interviewee's name, gender, country, and approximate age _____

_____

1. Look on this map. Where is *my country?* (For example, if you are from Guatemala, ask "Where is *Guatemala?*")

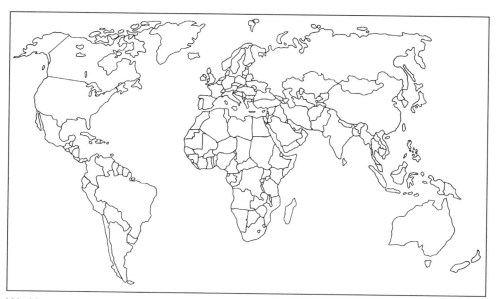

World map

2. *Q:* What do you know about *my country?*

    A: _____

    _____

    _____

    _____

3. *Q:* What is your impression of *my country?*

    A: _____

    _____

    _____

    _____

4. *Q:* Where did you get your impression?

    A: _____

5. *Q:* _Do you know any famous people from my country?_

    A: _____

    _____

    _____

    _____

6. *Q:* _____

    A: _____

    _____

    _____

7. *Q:* _____

    A: _____

    _____

    _____

8. Q: _____

    A: _____

    _____

    _____

    _____

9. Q: _____

    A: _____

    _____

    _____

    _____

10. Q: _____

    A: _____

    _____

    _____

    _____

11. Q: _____

    A: _____

    _____

    _____

    _____

12. Q: _____

    A: _____

    _____

    _____

    _____

13. Q: _____

    A: _____

    _____

    _____

14. Q: _____

    A: _____

    _____

    _____

15. Q: _____

    A: _____

    _____

    _____

After the Activity
· · · · · · · · · · · · · · · · · · · ·

1. In groups of four or five students, discuss your interviews.

2. Write two things that surprised you most during your interview.

    _____

    _____

3. Did the interviewee know more or less than you expected? _____

    _____

4. Did the American say anything that made you think of your country in a different way? If so, what, and why?

    _____

    _____

    _____

5. If you could teach everyone in the world one thing about your native country, what would it be?

    _____

6. Did you tell this to the person you interviewed? _____

7. The Greek root "xeno-" means *stranger* or *foreigner*. As a class, guess the meaning of the words "**xenophilia**" and "**xenophobia.**" Write your guesses. Then, check your answers at the end of this chapter.

    _____

    _____

8. Do you think that a person's knowledge or ignorance about a foreign country might contribute to being a xenophobe or xenophile? Explain your answer.

    _____

    _____

    _____

    _____

9. Do you know anybody who is xenophobic or xenophilic? If so, explain his or her views, if you can.

    _____

    _____

    _____

    _____

10. In your native language, do the words xenophobic and xenophilic exist? If so, write them down. If not, why, in your opinion, don't they exist?

    _____

    _____

Optional Activities

· · · · · · · · · · · · · · · · · · · ·

- If your class is multicultural, do your interview again. This time, interview a student who is not from your country.

- Ask the American whom you interviewed to create an interview about America. Answer his or her questions.

- In same-country groups (students from the same country), make a poster about your country. Hang it in your classroom.

- In same-country groups, make a presentation about your country. Offer to present it to your class, to a local community center, to another class, or to any other group that might be interested.

- Choose five to ten words from this chapter that are new for you. Write the words and write your own sentences using these words.

GLOSSARY

atlas, noun	A book of maps.
geography, noun	The descriptive science dealing with the surface of the earth.
xenophilia, noun	Attraction to or admiration of foreigners.
xenophobia, noun	The fear of strangers or foreigners.

Y

Your Activity

Insert a photo of you here!

Prep & Preview
· · · · · · · · · · · · · · · ·
You will design and implement an activity. You might want to work with a classmate.

Cost: Free/Varies according to student needs

Note: This activity should be done only after you have completed several other chapters in this book. It is not appropriate as a first activity.

Before the Activity
· · · · · · · · · · · · · · · · · · · ·

1. Think of three things in America that you have noticed but that seem somehow strange or unlike your own country. They should be things that you don't understand well. Write them here.

    _____

    _____

    _____

2. In pairs, discuss your ideas. Discuss different ways that you could research these through **observation,** reading, discussion with Americans, participation in some activity, or personal experience.

3. Choose one of the three ideas. It will be the focus of this chapter. Write it here. If another classmate is interested in the same topic, you might want to work together in pairs.

    _____

4. What have you observed in America on this topic that seems strange to you? Why does it seem strange?

    _____

    _____

    _____

5. Try to think of some of your basic beliefs, **assumption**s, or **habit**s on this topic. How is this topic/event dealt with in your country?

_____

_____

_____

_____

6. Where did you get your basic beliefs and assumptions?

_____

_____

_____

7. On the next page, plan an activity that would help you to learn more about this topic as it is viewed in America. (You might want to take notes on scratch paper first.) You may choose to go somewhere, to interview someone, to do library research, or so on. It's up to you.

8. Work in pairs or small groups. Help each other come up with ideas. Discuss your plans. Improve them.

The Activity
. . . .

This activity is to be completely planned, written, and completed by you. It might help you to use other activities in this book as a model.

_____

_____

_____

_____

_____

_____

_____

_____

_____

_____

_____

_____

_____

_____

CULTURE (You write this Culture Nugget) _____

NUGGET _____

_____

After the Activity

1. In large groups in your class, discuss your activity. First, tell your classmates what you researched. Then, tell them about your research. Tell them what you learned.

2. Listen to your classmates' experiences. Write the topics, research, and conclusions of three fellow students.

_____

_____

_____

_____

_____

_____

_____

_____

_____

3.   Write a one-page report about your experience. What did you learn? Staple it to this page.

4.   If you have an American friend or acquaintance, ask him or her to look at your report. Ask for their response.

Optional Activities
. . . .

•   Do this activity again on a different topic.

•   If your classmates did interesting research, ask them more about their work.

•   Imagine that an American comes to your native country. What things would likely be confusing or strange for him or her?

•   Imagine that an American comes to your native country and observes the same topic in your country that you researched for this chapter. What do you think the American would feel or conclude?

•   Look up the word "culture" in a dictionary. Write down the definition.

•   In your opinion, which has had a greater influence on your life and beliefs: your parents or your culture? Of course, parents transmit culture. However, try to consider the unique roles of each. In large groups, discuss this idea.

- Choose five to ten words from this chapter that are new for you. Write the words and write your own sentences using these words.

GLOSSARY

assumption, noun	Something that a person thinks but does not know.
habit, noun	Something that is done regularly without thinking about it.
observation, noun	Something you have noticed by watching carefully.

Z

Zoo

Central Park Zoo is a popular zoo located in the center of New York City.

Prep & Preview You will go to a nearby zoo (or aquarium or aviary).
. . . . Cost: Zoo entrance fee, which varies.

Note: This activity can easily be adapted for an aquarium or an aviary.

Before the Activity
. . . .

1. What is your favorite animal and why? _____
    _____

2. What's your least favorite animal and why? _____
    _____

3. If you could be an animal besides a human, what would you be? _____

4. Look at these words. If you know them, write what they mean. (Some of
    these words may sound the same in your language as in English.)

    arachnid   _____

    aviary   _____

    aquarium   _____

    mammal   _____

    primate   _____

    reptile   _____

    vertebrate   _____

5. In small groups, talk about your answers to the above questions. Try to get
    the meaning of all of the words in task 4.

6. Choose one animal group in task 4 that interests you most. Circle it. Talk to
    your classmates. If somebody chose the same animal group that you chose,
    you may want to work together on this activity. It would be best to work
    with a student who has a different native language from yours.

7. Read through the activity that follows. Make sure that you understand it. You may work with a classmate, or ask your teacher if you have questions.

The Activity
. . . .

1. Call the zoo, aquarium, or aviary in your area and ask about their hours. Name the type of animal that interests you most, and ask if there are special tours of that section in the zoo. What time(s) are the tours?

    Zoo name _____   Zoo phone _____

    Zoo hours _____   Special section tours _____

    Zoo entrance fee _____   Zoo address _____

2. Go to the zoo. Go to the section of the zoo that especially interests you. If the zoo has special tours of that section, take that tour.

3. If you go with classmates, write their names here _____

    _____

4. Paste your zoo ticket here.

5. Find one specific animal that interests you and find out the following information about it.

    a. Name of animal _____

    b. How long do they usually live? _____

    c. How many **offspring** might they have? _____

    d. Where do they live naturally? _____

    e. What do they eat? _____

    f. Can they smell, see, and hear?_____

    g. Can they go up a tree, swim, or fly? _____

    h. Where did the zoo get this particular animal? _____

    i.   How much did it cost the zoo to buy that animal? _____

    j.   (Your question) _____?

_____

    k.   (Your question) _____?

_____

    l.   (Your question) _____?

_____

6.   If you have a camera, take a picture of the animal. Paste it here.

7.   If the zoo has a brochure, take one and attach it to this page.

8.   Did you see any animals at the zoo that you have never seen before?

9.   Did you notice anything of special interest at the zoo?

After the Activity

1.   In large groups, share the information that you learned about your animal with your classmates. Show them any pictures you took of animals.

2.   Listen to your classmates' information.

3. Write the names of three animals that your classmates researched. Write something that you learned about each animal.

---

4. Talk about your general zoo experience. How was the American zoo different from zoos in your country? How was it similar?

5. Talk about other zoos, aquariums, or aviaries that you have visited in the United States, in your country, or in another country. Compare the information you have with your classmates'.

CULTURE NUGGET The Bronx Zoo, in New York City, is one of the largest and most successful zoos in the United States. It has more than 4,200 wild animals. The animals live in areas that are similar to their natural **habitat**s rather than in **pen**s. The most popular building is the reptile house. (Joyce Altman and Sue Goldberg, *Dear Bronx Zoo* [New York: Macmillan Publishing Company, 1990].)

Optional Activities

• • • • • • • • • • • • • • • • • • • •

• Go to the library and read about the animal that you are most interested in. Learn something more about the animal. Add the information you found to this book.

- Go to a pet store. Are any pets sold there that in your country are a wild animal?

- Watch a TV program about animals on a National Geographic special or on the Discovery Channel (if you have cable TV), or on your local public station.

- In the library, find a book on zoos in the children's section. Learn the English words for five animals that you don't already know. Bring the book to class. Teach the words to your classmates.

- Go back to the zoo, or go to an aquarium or aviary. Learn about another animal.

- Choose five to ten words from this chapter that are new for you. Write the words and write your own sentences using these words.

GLOSSARY	
habitat, noun	The place where something naturally lives.
offspring, noun	Animal young; children.
pen, noun	A small enclosed area for animals.